ACCRINGTON'S
PUBLIC TRANSPORT
1886 – 1986

by

Robert W. Rush

Landy Publishing
2000

ISBN 1 872895 53 0

British Library in Cataloguing Publication Data
A catalogue record of this book is available from the British Library.

Layout by Mike Clarke. Tel/Fax: 01254 395848

Printed by Nayler the Printer Ltd, Accrington. Tel: 01254 234247

Landy Publishing have also published:

An Accrington Mixture edited by Bob Dobson
Accrington Observed compiled by Brian Brindle & Bob Dobson
Accrington's Changing Face compiled by Frank Watson & Bob Dobson
Rishton Remembered by Kathleen Broderick
Lancashire This, That an't'other by Doris Snape
Lancashire Lingo Lines dialect poetry edited by Bob Dobson
Lancashire Bonds; Poems & Monologues by Alan & Les Bond
A Blackburn Miscellany edited by Bob Dobson
Blackburn Tram Rides by Jim Halsall
Blackburn In Times Gone By compiled by Jim Halsall
Clitheroe Ablaze With Glory by Sue Holden
The Moorfield Pit Disaster by Harry Tootle

A full list is available from:
Landy Publishing
'Acorns', 3 Staining Rise, Staining,
Blackpool FY3 0BU
Tel/Fax 01253 895678

Accrington celebrates the Coronation in June 1902 in some style. There is no photograph of the town looking busier. The steam trams are jostling for space with traders' horse-drawn vehicles, handcarts and pedestrians. In the immediate foreground the tub on the handcart is full of — this is on the best of authority — ice cream. How many other photos show men on the Town Hall roof? Controlling all this bustle and activity is a policeman on point duty.

No. 43 stands on the middle track in Peel Street, ready to proceed to Oswaldtwistle. The end of the roof of the Gordon shelter is just visible at the front of the tram. This was one of the pair of cars (42 & 43) of special low built construction to pass under the railway bridge at Church station. Later one of them worked to Blackburn fairly often, as there was a similar low bridge near Blythe's Chemical works, Church.

Not a motor vehicle in sight, just two steam trams and two horses, as we look up Little Blackburn Road at the turn of the century. Woods' tobacconists were to move from this location further along Blackburn Road to the junction with Broadway.

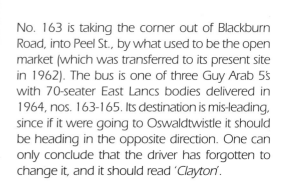

No. 163 is taking the corner out of Blackburn Road, into Peel St., by what used to be the open market (which was transferred to its present site in 1962). The bus is one of three Guy Arab 5's with 70-seater East Lancs bodies delivered in 1964, nos. 163-165. Its destination is mis-leading, since if it were going to Oswaldtwistle it should be heading in the opposite direction. One can only conclude that the driver has forgotten to change it, and it should read *Clayton*.

INTRODUCTION

In 1961 my original book on the *Tramways of Accrington* was published. This has long been out of print, and I decided I would write an abridged version of it, adding a short section on the buses which replaced the trams. Some additional data has has been added, while at the same time some minor errors have been corrected.

The opening of completely new electric tramways in Manchester and Sheffield, also proposals to introduce similar routes in Birmingham, Liverpool, and elsewhere appear to have re-awakened general interest. There is no mistaking the capability of electric tramcars for moving large numbers of people from place to place with the minimum of fuss, and with no pollution of the atmosphere, though the overhead wiring is regarded in some quarters as unsightly. This system of supplying electric current to the vehicles has been recognised as the most efficient, and easiest to construct, unlike the conduit system formerly used in London, or the 'livestuds' between the rails used for some years in Lincoln, Wolverhampton, Torquay, and other places, which were expensive to construct, and unreliable in service (not to mention dangerous!).

It has been mentioned in the local press that consideration is being given to the re-introduction of tramways in East Lancashire, but in my own opinion I hardly think that it is feasible, for the bulk of our roads are not wide enough to accommodate a tram track in addition to the enormous amount of motor traffic these days. The alternative of trolley buses is much more likely, since they, like the motor bus, can move almost anywhere within the road width, if necessary. They also have the advantage of being almost silent in operation, and do not emit clouds of noxious fumes. I think a trolley bus network would be a great advantage. Countless thousands might disagree.

Anyway, we must leave this question with the 'powers that be', and abide by their conclusions, but I have no hesitation in saying that almost anything would be better than the present chaotic 'bus set-up.

Unfortunately, to remember Accrington's trams one must be at least seventy years of age, and there aren't all that many of us left. However, I hope this book will stir some memories among the old folk, and prove of interest to some of the 'youngsters' as well.

My sincere thanks are due to the late Walter Gratwicke, Jim Halsall, Jeff Duckworth, Roy Maudsley, Fred Moore and especially Alan Parkin for the use of photographs.

I thank the National Tramways Museum librarian, Glynn Wilton for his assistance. I am also grateful to the Accrington Local Studies librarians Catherine Duckworth and Helen Barrett for the use of their photographs and for allowing me to study the minutes of the Accrington Tramways and Transport Committees. I thank June Huntingdon and Mike Clarke for their help at the typing and typesetting stage.

Robert W Rush

Robert W Rush
February 2000

A very old photograph, date unknown, showing a steam tram at the Church terminus, the corner of Market Street. The house on the very corner in later years became a doctor's surgery, and was in use continually until the early 1960's at least. Apart from this, the row of buildings has changed only in minor details until this day. The reason for the crowd of people is conjectural; maybe they are waiting to board the car – the engine is not in evidence, possibly having gone off to turn round, and the passengers would not be allowed aboard until the engine was coupled on again. Notice the Post Office, with the telephone facility.

THE STEAM ERA

Localised public transport in Accrington was first mooted in 1882, when The Accrington Corporation Steam Tramways Company was founded. It was to some extent a joint undertaking, the Corporation being responsible for the laying and maintenance of the track-work, while the company would provide the rolling stock and work the services. There were to be three routes, radiating from the Market Place to Clayton, Church and Baxenden, a total of $5^1/_2$ miles. Work began in 1884 on the preparation of the roads to take the new steel rails, entailing much digging and laying of concrete to provide a solid base. This caused much inconvenience to the horse-drawn traffic of the time, and to the public at large, though it was accepted as being 'all in a good cause'. With much noise, dust, and heaving around of thousands of granite paving setts, the prodigious task was at last completed, and on 5th April 1886 it passed the vigorous Board of Trade inspection, and was ready for public service.

Steamed Up and Rolling

To operate the tramways, nine four-wheeled steam tramway engines were bought from the makers, Thomas Green & Sons of Leeds, along with ten double-deck, eight-wheeled passenger cars, built by the Falcon Engine & Car Works of Loughborough (the firm later to become the Brush Electrical Engineering Co). These cars had all enclosed upper decks, with drop windows in the sides, which could be opened to disperse the fog of smoke from countless clay pipes burning black twist, the favourite choice of the hoi-polloi who were expected to use the cars. Smoking was forbidden in the lower deck, where the ladies were supposed to ride, so these windows were fixed. At each end was an open platform, with an iron stairway to give access to the upper deck. Seating was lengthwise in both decks, the lower one being down each side with a central gangway, while upstairs they were arranged back to back along the centre, with a gangway at each side. Sixty passengers in all could be seated, plus as many as could find standing room, there being no hard and fast rule in those days to count the number of standing passengers, so quite often up to a hundred bodies could be accommodated at any one time.

In the evening of the opening day a celebration dinner was organised at the Commercial Hotel. It was presided over by Mr Cosh, managing director of the London firm of caterers who were responsible for the proceedings. About fifty persons attended, including the Mayor (Alderman Smith), members and officials of the Borough Council with representatives of the Church, Oswaldtwistle and Clayton local authorities. Mr Cramp, managing director of the Tramways Company was also present, with five members of the joint managing committee. A Mr Rowley represented the makers of the tramway engines, Thos. Green & Sons.

Beginning the after-dinner round of speeches, the chairman, Mr Cosh, proposed the toast to the 'Mayor and Corporation of Accrington', remarking that since coming to the town at the beginning of the negotiations for the tramways, he had been very kindly treated by the Corporation, and indeed by many members of the local public, for which he was very grateful. He felt very sure that everyone concerned had done their best for the townspeople, and that the tramways would prove a boon to them all.

In reply, the Mayor thanked everyone for the toast, and the generous remarks that had been made, said that Mr Cramp's conduct with the Corporation had been exemplary, and he hoped their attitude to him had been equally acceptable. They were all glad to see the hopes of the town consummated at last, in the new tramways. He was very pleased indeed to propose the toast of 'The Accrington Steam Tramways Company'.

Responding to the toast, Mr Cramp thanked everyone for the generous remarks which had been made. He gave it as his opinion that the tramways would prove a little gold mine, to the benefit of

'OL 2U2', the last working steam tram in the country, taking part in the 1928 Accrington Jubilee celebrations. It is pictured passing the Co-op in Abbey Street. It was retained, based at the Haslingden tram shed, and fitted with a snow plough for the winter's snow clearing operations.

The noise of the tram as it steamed down Whalley Road towards the town centre startled a horse drawing a cart out of Kenyon Street into Maudsley Street, seen here. The cart and the engine collided, resulting in damage to the garden wall of the end house in Britcliffe Row, and the engine coming off the rails. Some of the lads are carrying 'brew cans'.

all concerned. He said that steam tramways opened in the whole country up to the end of June 1885 had totalled 811 miles, and a total capital of £17 million had been raised. The cost of the Accrington tramways had been £30,000, plus £15,000 for engines and other equipment. Brought down to basics, this worked out at £8,263 per mile, which compared very favourably with the average cost per mile of other tramways, which was £13,483. They had calculated that allowing nine pence per mile for working expenses (which was the average cost), the tramways should make a net profit of £2,570 per annum, which would pay 10% on ordinary and preference shareholdings. The company had every desire to work closely with the Council and townspeople, and they hoped the tramways would be a great success.

Further toasts were drunk to the Tramways Committee, the town and traders of Accrington, and the neighbouring townships of Church, Oswaldtwistle, and Clayton. Finally the Chairman, the Borough Officials, and the Press were all toasted, and the proceedings ended with the singing of the National Anthem.

In course of time, as the tramways progressed and became more popular, a further nine engines were purchased from Green's at intervals between 1888 to 1898, and seven more passenger cars, though these came from two different makers, the Ashbury Carriage & Iron Company of Manchester, and the Lancaster Railway Carriage & Wagon Company, of the same general design, but with minor differences according to the maker's practice. The Lancaster carriages had what were termed *'garden seats'* with reversible backs upstairs arranged for two on each seat, along the sides with a central gangway. The ends of the cars had windows to prevent the ingress of soot and sparks from the tall engine chimneys.

Finally, four second hand Green engines were purchased for next to nothing from Blackburn Corporation in 1901, bringing the total to 22, but some of the earlier engines must have been withdrawn, for in 1907 there were stated to be only eleven engines in service.

Southbound

The extension of the line from Baxenden to the centre of Haslingden was opened on 27th August 1887, and completed to the Haslingden/Rawtenstall boundary at Lockgate on 18 November of the same year. This extension was owned by Haslingden Corporation, who agreed to lay the track and maintain it, but were quite content to allow the Accrington company to work it. The total mileage was now increased to $9^1/_2$ miles. At Lockgate the track joined end-on to the Rossendale Steam Tramways Co.; likewise at Church, the Accrington lines joined those of Blackburn Corporation, but in neither case was any through running ever established. The steam tramways were regarded by many as noisy, filthy, slow and uncomfortable, but the majority were glad of the service they provided, and were sorry to see them go eventually.

On 5th July 1900 a steam tram (no.6) of Blackburn Corporation made a through run from Darwen to Bacup, via Accrington and

A special trip from Darwen to Bacup, with various officials from the Corporations, 5th July, 1900. Blackburn car, no.6, at the corner of Accrington Market Place.

Rawtenstall, a distance of about 20 miles, the tracks of four different operators being involved. This was the official farewell to the Blackburn steam tramways, for the electrification of their system had just been completed. The steam car made ceremonial stops at each town passed en route, with the usual speeches, and a dinner held at the Commercial Hotel, Accrington, where the whole assembly of officials and dignitaries was photographed. After this, they stopped at Haslingden, Rawtenstall and Waterfoot, finally reaching Bacup in about 4¹/₂ hours, of which just over two hours was actual running time. At Bacup the entourage turned round and returned to Blackburn, with brief stops to set down officials en route. This gentle hint on the part of Blackburn Corporation for the possibilities of through running in the future was, unfortunately, never taken up in earnest.

Brass Talks

A piece written in the Automotor Journal of March 25th 1905 gives an insight into the thinking on publicly-financed transport at a time when the town's trams had not yet started to run on electricity but a good deal of Town Hall money had been spent on bringing it about.

"*They do things apparently on somewhat peculiar principles in Accrington. In that town they possess an electric lighting concern,*

to which a contract for supplying current for electric tramways would doubtless come in handy. The Corporation of the town, after spending a large sum on the electrification of the tramways, turned its attention to the motor 'bus question . In order to procure an 'unprejudiced' opinion on the situation for their guidance, they appear to have requested the chairman of the electric light undertaking to report to them his views on the motor 'bus question. This gentleman needless to say, reports his conclusion that electric cars are much to be preferred. He adds further observations about speed, the smell of petrol, &c., and we are informed, in addition, that he is an experienced motorist. But the 'argumentum ad pocketum' seems to have prevailed".

Gone but not Forgotten

Here's a couplet written at the time of the 'passing' of the steam trams

IN LOVING MEMORY
Weep not for me, my life is past
Dearly you loved me to the last,
Grieve not, dear friends, but continue kind
To the Electric Cars I leave behind.

The last steam tram to run on the Baxenden route on 28th September 1887. This is engine no. 2 with car no. 10.

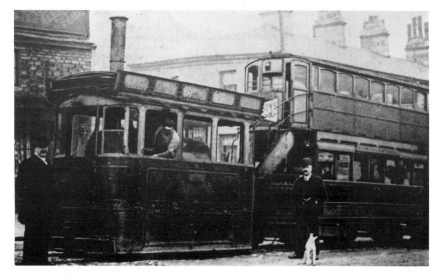

We have busy Accrington photographer Mr Constantine to thank for capturing this moment in our history. The Whalley Road/ Blackburn Road crossing at Clayton, some time before 1907, since a steam tram is seen hurtling towards Accrington. The *Hare & Hounds* pub is seen on the left and the *Load of Mischief* is just off the picture on the right… what appears to be a Corporation road-sweeper's cart, with its crew, is in front of the *Hare & Hounds*, while on the other side a horse-drawn van is turning out of Blackburn Road into Whalley Road.

Even if this photograph was not dated 17th September 1907, the erection of the Accrington & Church Co-operative Society's fine emporium *'Croft House'* would provide a clue, for it was opened for business in February 1908. The new-fangled electric trams are causing interest to the pedestrians and young chap with his up-to-the-minute bicycle. Croft House replaced a fine early Victorian house of the same name on that site, which stretched down Oxford Street to Blake Street. Formerly it had been called Vicar Street, and that was certainly a reference to St. James' Church vicarage, which stood in Ellison Street alongside the site. That vicarage would later be used as the offices for the Corporation's Transport Department.

TRIAL TRIP OF TWO DECKER CAR ACCRINGTON SEPT. 17. 1907.

Burnley Road, Accrington

Photographs of trams on Burnley Road are scarce. No.6 is on its way from the Cemetery to the town centre, passing Addison Street and Windsor Street.

THE ELECTRIC ERA

Tramway legislation laid down that after 21 years from the opening date, the steam tramways in any municipal area could be purchased by the relevant municipal authority, and if the option was not taken up then, it could be renewed for further periods of seven years each. So in 1907 Accrington Corporation decided to take up the option to purchase, and convert the system to electric working. After much argument between the two sides — eventually going to arbitration — the Corporation purchased the entire undertaking for £2,227, and proceeded to relay the trackwork and erect the necessary overhead wiring and other equipment in readiness for electric working. As regards the Haslingden section, Haslingden Corporation agreed to continue the existing conditions — they would pay for the electrification, but were quite content to let Accrington continue the working.

Work Begins

Work began early in 1907 on relaying the track with heavier rails, and putting in the electrical bonding at rail joints (un-necessary with steam working) also the erection of the lineside standards and their attendant wiring. The opportunity was taken to modify the track layout in certain places to improve the working, and to put in a few extra passing loops to speed up the services. The chief alteration was to the Baxenden line, for in steam days trams in both directions used the same single track from the top of Blackburn Road to the Market Place, which was very inconvenient. It was decided to change the outward route to go via Peel Street, turning right at the top into Abbey Street, and so joining the original route at the top of Blackburn Road. Inward cars would continue to use Blackburn Road to reach the Market, and would continue along Blackburn Road for 250 yards to the railway viaduct, where they would reverse, and return to the Market Place. The Clayton cars would also reverse at the viaduct, to avoid an awkward manoeuvre at the Market. Some passing loops were also to be lengthened from the standard 45 feet, where a slight bend in the road occurred.

Fresh Territory

Two new routes were also taken in hand, one up Burnley Road to the cemetery gates, and the other an extension from Church, round the sharp corner into Market Street, and up Union Road to a new terminus at the *Black Dog Inn*, Oswaldtwistle. These would add a further $2^1/_2$ miles to the system. The Clayton route was also extended by 600 yards from the old terminus at the *Load of Mischief Hotel* to the bridge over the Leeds and Liverpool canal. The route to Oswaldtwistle was far from easy, since Union Road was not very wide and was rather tortuous, so single track with passing loops was a necessity.

Cost Conscious

It is interesting to take a look at the hidden costs of opening an electric tramway. The necessary electric current had to be paid for, in spite of the fact that the Corporation also owned the power station. A fee of one and a half (old) pence per unit was arrived at for this. Tickets had to be purchased from the printers. The Corporation forgot this, and a hurried order had to be put in at the last moment. Uniforms were necessary for the staff; these were obtained on contract from a firm in Derby. Tunics cost 19 shillings each, trousers 10 shillings 6 pence, overcoats 24 shillings 6 pence, and caps 3 shillings 6 pence, a total of 2 pounds, 17 shillings 6 pence (£2.87$^1/_2$) for each outfit. Even for 1907, these prices seem rather low, but they were certainly of good quality — no shoddy material was countenanced by the Corporation.

Wages were another item not to be sneezed at. Inspectors were paid 28 shillings per week (£1.40) drivers 27 shillings (£1.35) conductors 22 shillings 6 pence (£1.12$^1/_2$) and cleaners 27 shillings (£1.35). Cleaners worked a 59$^1/_2$ hour week, whilst the rest of the staff worked a nine hour day. There were also a host of ancilliary workers — clerks, mechanics, electricians, carpenters, painters, track and paving workers and others, who constituted the office and depot staff.

Tram Sheds

The old steam tram depot in Ellison Street was retained, with some alterations, including a new workshop and paint shop added at the rear. This sufficed until 1909, when, owing to the addition of new cars to the fleet, it became somewhat overcrowded, and a new extension was proposed. There was plenty of room for this, since adjoining the depot was a very large tract of open ground, known as *'Ellisons Tenement'*, which from time immemorial had housed the town's twice yearly fun fairs. Plans were drawn up, and the work started in 1912. It had not been completed when war broke out in August 1914, and had to be held in abeyance. The new extension to the depot did not come into use until 1919.

In 1907/8 the old steam stock was gathered in and put on some temporary track on Ellison's Tenement, where it was sorted out and broken up for scrap by the firm of T. W. Ward & Co of Sheffield. On the whole, the Corporation came out of this transaction very well, for in spite of having to pay out £2,227 for the old tramway, they received £1,230 from Ward's for the scrap, and also 63 shillings (£3.30) per ton for the old rails, which also went for scrap, and more than recouped their outlay.

We're Off!! (Off Their Trolley?)

The opening ceremony on 2nd August 1907 began with a procession of the four single deck cars, driven by the Mayoress, the Deputy

Tram No. 4 at Hillock Vale by the cemetery, the terminus for the Burnley Road section. It was planned to extend it to the Griffin Hotel at Huncoat, but this never happened. Behind the wall is a reservoir, which is now filled in, houses built on the land. This was the last route to close on January 6th, 1932.

Mayoress, Mrs Aitken (wife of the Town Clerk) and Mrs Bury (wife of the leader of the Council) under the supervision of the regular drivers. The entourage left the depot, loaded with members of the Town Council and other officials, and proceeded to Oswaldtwistle. Blackburn sent one of their large single deck cars, and Darwen a small, one-man, single decker to tag onto the rear of the procession. These two, however, could not go beyond Church, as their trolley standards were too high for the bridge at Church station, so they had to wait at Church until the procession returned. For the uninitiated, the term 'trolley standard' needs explanation. The trolley, or boom, which was used to collect current from the overhead wires was a circular section wooden pole, about 15 to 20 feet long, with a metal wheel at the end to connect with the wire. The lower end was mounted in a metal frame, fitted with (usually) two springs, to maintain a continuous contact with the overhead wire. The whole was mounted on the roof of the tramcar, and could be swivelled round in a complete circle, so that it would follow the wire, and could always be maintained in a trailing direction. Some designers preferred not to fit the trolley boom directly to the roof of the car, and so used a short length — usually three or four feet — of iron piping about eight to nine inches in diameter fastened to the roof, and the trolley boom mounted on top of it – this arrangement was known as the 'trolley standard'. It must be pointed out that a standard was specified by law for use in the case of open topped cars (i.e. with seats on the roof) so that passengers did not come into contact with the trolley boom. Usually, with open topped cars, the trolley standard was mounted in the centre, but in some cases (like Blackburn) where the overhead wires were carried on short brackets from the top of the tall standards which carried them, the trolley standard had to be fixed to one side instead, in order to avoid too great an angle between the trolley base and the overhead wire. These were known as 'side-running trolleys'.

Red Faces

Several speeches were made, by the Mayor and other officials at the Oswaldtwistle terminus, to the acclamation of the people present. The procession then returned to Ellison Street. It had been intended to run through to the Town Hall, but an unexplained fault

in the overhead gear suddenly developed, and the cars could not proceed beyond Ellison Street. So the dignitaries had to walk the three hundred yards or so to the Town Hall. The Mayor addressed the crowd from the balcony and declared the tramways open – though public services did not begin until two days later. This time there was no celebratory dinner, as was the case when the steam tramways were opened in 1886.

The Routes Described

1: Burnley Road Route

Always the Cinderella of the system, its comparative failure was due to the fact that it was never extended to its logical conclusion — the village of Huncoat. It stopped short at the cemetery gates, admittedly a hundred yards or so inside the Parish of Huncoat, but from there to the Griffin's Head Hotel the fairly wide, straight road had nothing on it but Spout House Farm and two or three widely separated cottages in its quarter mile length. The village of Huncoat — a fairly large community — really began at the Griffin, and extended for quite a distance along an unclassified road, down to the railway station, which was the logical terminus for a tram route. The possibility of extending it to the station was discussed several times, but the Council seemed to be deterred by the quarter mile of empty road between the cemetery and the Griffin. When it was decided to do something, the 1914 war intervened, effectively putting paid to the project. Huncoat had no public transport (apart from the railway) until a bus service was begun late in 1928.

Though Burnley Road was completely built up with housing right up to the cemetery, the route only really paid its way on Saturdays, when there was a football or cricket match on, as both grounds, about a quarter mile apart, were just off Burnley Road. On those days, there was a continual procession of trams up and down the road, filled with eager spectators, some cars running through from Oswaldtwistle, Clayton, or Baxenden. These were the only occasions when double deck cars were used on Burnley Road.

From the Market Hall, the line ran up the short length of Peel Street, then turned left into Whalley Road, and in eighty yards turned off again to the right into Burnley Road itself. The track was double through this section as far as Melbourne Street, fifty yards from the bottom of Burnley Road; from here it was single all the way to the terminus, with passing loops at Cambridge Street; Alice Street, and the Cemetery Hotel. Alice Street was the stop for Peel Park football ground, and the Cemetery Hotel the stop for the cricket ground. There were no important buildings on this route, only terraced housing, with a few scattered shops.

I Get The Fever

For the first eleven years of my life, from 1912 to 1923, I lived at 203 Burnley Road, right opposite to Alice Street. Lying in bed at night, I well remember hearing the last tram of the day (11 p.m. from the cemetery) on its journey down the road. It used to travel at a speed well in excess of the statutory 12 mph, and in the dead quiet of those days at that time of night, I could hear the 'thud, thud' of the wheels passing the rail joints, and the clatter as it went through the points at the loops all the way from the terminus to the bottom of Burnley Road. Very very rarely did that tram stop during the whole length of its journey. I could pin-point the actual position of that tram at any time.

Early in 1917, when I was about $4^1/_2$ years old, my mother's sister, Katherine Roney (*'Aunt Kate'*), enrolled as a conductress on the trams, being one of the very first. One morning I was happily playing by myself in the front garden when a tram stopped outside. Aunt Kate dashed in, grabbed me, and dumped me in the rear corner of the tram seat, and I got an extended ride, to the cemetery, all the way back to Oswaldtwistle, and finally home again. I was AWOL for about an hour and when Aunt Kate dropped me off at the house, there was an awful row. My grandmother severely castigated Aunt Kate for kidnapping me. There was pandemonium when my absence was discovered, leading to a thorough search of the rambling house, its 50-yard long back garden, and the large cellar. They had just decided to contact the police when Aunt Kate returned me to the fold. Subsequently an arrangement was worked out, whereby Aunt Kate could pick me up and take me for a tram ride when she was on that particular turn, and the family would know where I was. This arrangement didn't last very long, however, as in the following September I started school, so my jaunts were

severely curtailed. They did not cease entirely until 1919, When Aunt Kate retired from conductorising. It was due to Aunt Kate that I began my great interest in electric tramways as a whole, and later led to a similar profound interest in railways.

The Dead End Routes

For a number of years the Corporation hired out a single deck tram for funeral parties going to the cemetery. This led to a profound animosity between the Corporation and the North East Lancashire Carriage Proprietors Association, who looked upon the hiring of tram cars for funerals as being well outside the Corporation's terms of reference. Arguments between the two sides were many, but not until the motor car became an alternative to the horse carriage in 1922, did the funeral cars cease to run.

Burnley Road, though the least profitable route by far, was actually the last to remain in use, outliving the other routes by four months, as there were not sufficient motor buses to take over. It closed on 6th January 1932, no. 6 being the very last tram to run in Accrington — making its final journey with a large dent in one dashplate.

2: Clayton Route

From the Market Place, the cars proceeded up Peel Street, turning left into Whalley Road, going straight on past the Burnley Road junction. The road was level as far as the Castle Hotel, but then began a stiffish rise, under the railway viaduct, for almost a mile to Oakleigh. From here to the Clayton terminus was mostly downhill, with a lengthy level stretch between the Greyhound and Load of Mischief hotels. On the way the route passed the Victoria Hospital, at the junction with Queen's Road, and here the continuous double track from the Market ended. For the rest of the way the line was single, with passing loops, except for the final 600 yards from the Load of Mischief to the terminus. The loops were situated at Oakleigh, the Crown Inn (an elongated one this, as there was a slight bend in the road) and at Sydney Street, Clayton, about half way between the Greyhound and Load of Mischief pubs. At the Greyhound the route crossed the boundary into the Urban District of Clayton-le-Moors.

As far as Oakleigh, the housing was typically urban, mainly terraced houses, with a few shops, but onwards to the Greyhound

No. 40 stands in Peel Street at four o'clock. The ladies on the pavement have been shopping on the market. This was one of the four all-enclosed double-decked trams obtained in 1919/20 chiefly for the Clayton-Accrington-Church service. They were used mainly only on Saturdays and Sundays, but did appear occasionally on other days for peak-time service.

Photo by W. Gratwicke

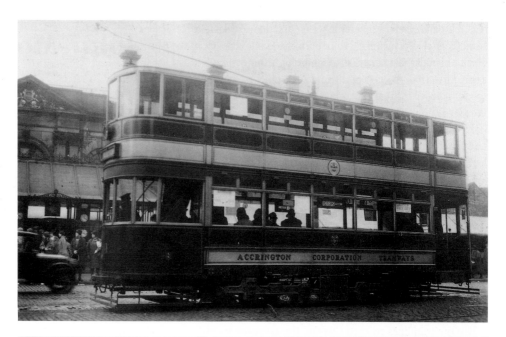

Single-decker No. 5, with the driver open to the elements, on its way from Church to Accrington about 1910. The shops on the right are between China and India Streets.

(Church Lane) there were a number of large houses, some three-storied, many of which have since been made into flats. From the Clayton boundary at Church Lane, the housing became typically urban again. Apart from the hospital, there were no other establishments of special note, apart from three churches:- Whalley Road Methodist, Whalley Road Congregational and St. Mary Magdalene's. Just before Oakleigh, the road skirted the edge of Laneside housing estate. In 1968, just behind the Crown Inn, Accrington Stanley F.C. set up its new football ground as a non-league side; resurrected from the ashes of the original Stanley who were expelled from the Football League in 1962. The Clayton route was closed, along with the other lines to Church and Oswaldtwistle, on 26 August 1931, the replacement bus service running through between Clayton and Oswaldtwistle. Fares from Accrington were Owen Street (1d), Oakleigh (1½d), Church Lane (2d), Load of Mischief (2½d) and 3d to the terminus. These fares had applied unaltered for a number of years — certainly since the end of the First World War.

Clayton gets on the Map

When the tramlines reached Clayton, the 'favourite vocalist and author', Jerry Morgan, wrote a celebratory song, which was printed locally and sold as a 'penny reading'. The chorus went:-

Then oh, what jolly fun, the time at last has come
When we can ride upon the tram as far as Accrington;
Only twopence is the fare, we can very soon be there
Now we've got a tram to run to Clayton.

3: Church and Oswaldtwistle Route

This was the second most profitable line — Clayton holding the prime position. It was double tracked for the whole of its length to Church, with three crossovers at strategic points — Ellison Street, the Grammar School, and Lonsdale Street for emergency use. There was also a crossover at the railway viaduct, where the Clayton and Rawtenstall cars regularly reversed, and another in front of the Market Hall, for the Blackburn cars. In 1924, this latter was removed, as it presented difficulties for the Blackburn cars, which had to travel 50 yards round the corner from their terminus in the middle of the three-road layout at the Market Place, on the wrong line to the crossover. When the market stalls were in use, this

rendered the corner a blind one, and it is remarkable that the layout was not altered sooner. The crossover was re-sited in the Market Place, between the middle and outer lines.

Leaving the Market Place the line turned immediately right, into Blackburn Road, passing the front of the Market Hall and Town Hall, to the railway viaduct, then about a hundred yards further. Ellison Street was reached, a short descent on the right taking the line to the depot. Here a triangular junction was laid in, so that cars coming from the depot could proceed in either direction without reversal. It was also useful for turning a car end for end, if necessary. (Chiefly to ensure that the side-mounted trolleys for the Blackburn cars were on the correct side). In another three hundred yards, the Grammar School was seen on the right hand side, a very imposing, three storey building, with basement. Soon afterwards, on the opposite side of the road, the Church of the Sacred Heart, the main Roman Catholic church of the town, was passed. From here to Church there were no other establishments of note, except St. Andrews Church in Swiss Street, which was just visible from Blackburn Road.

From t'Commercial

At Church, close by the pub known as 'Church Commercial' the line made an end-on junction with Blackburn Corporation's route from that town, four miles away. A double junction was put in here, turning left into Market Street, and passing under the railway at Church Station, by a bridge with only 14ft 9in headroom, which meant that only single deck cars could be used. From here the track was single all the way up Union Road to the Oswaldtwistle terminus at The Black Dog pub, with loops at the Palladium cinema, Oswaldtwistle Town Hall, Rhyddings Street, and the Library. At first the loops were all of the standard length, but later the first two were lengthened to go round bends. Previously it was not possible to see one loop from the other.

This was the principal trouble with Union Road, and during the first few months of working there were several minor collisions on the lengths of single track because drivers could not see whether the sections were occupied by another car. A system of colour light signals was introduced early in 1908 to show the drivers whether or not the single line sections were occupied, and there were no more collisions.

Union Road was typical of the small industrial town with rows of terraced housing interspersed with shops, a few public houses, and the same official buildings — Town Hall, Fire Station, and

Outside the Ellison Street tram depot. A single deck electric tram, decorated for Accrington Shopping Festival Week, September 1910. It was one way of advertising local events around the town.

No. 2 is on its way to Accrington, and is here passing Church & Oswaldtwistle Railway Station.

No.4 is perhaps showing *'Depot'* as its destination because this was a trial run in 1907 to test the equipment on a first run to Oswaldtwistle. On both views we see other forms of transport.

the Public Library, and two or three churches. It would perhaps have been advantageous to have extended the line about a quarter mile further, to tap the suburban village of Stanhill, but apparently this was never contemplated.

The route was always extremely well patronised, and probably had more 'extra' cars working on it at peak periods than any other route. On Saturdays and Sundays double deck cars ran through from Clayton to Church.

Writing on the Wall

In the autumn of 1930 Oswaldtwistle U.D.C. consulted Accrington Corporation concerning the roadway in Union Road, which was in a very bad condition and in need of urgent reconstruction. After some lengthy consultation, the two authorities agreed that it would be best to close the tramway entirely, rather than having two major upheavals, the reconstruction of the road and a scrapping of the tramway at some not-far-off date in the future. The Rawtenstall route had already gone, losing Accrington half of its operations, and thus the writing was on the wall for the rest of the system. So it was agreed that the Oswaldtwistle line should be closed when the reconstruction works began, on 26th August 1931.

Left with only the Clayton and Burnley Road routes, the Corporation decided that the entire system might as well close on the same date. There was however, the question of the through route to Blackburn, which would be severed if the section to Church was closed. There were three options – close it down, sell the Church section to Blackburn Corporation (who probably would have bought it willingly) or to maintain it themselves. They did not like the idea of maintaining one mile of double track and four cars (nos. 11, 24, 42 and 43) to keep the through service running, so, reluctantly, it was decided to close the Church section as well. As things turned out, Blackburn Corporation kept their route from Church right to the end, in September 1949.

4: Baxenden Route

This was the most difficult of the four routes to work, since for almost all of its $2\frac{1}{4}$ miles, it was steadily uphill, a total rise of 260 feet, ending in a summit near Baxenden station at 730 feet above sea level. The road was reasonably wide for those days, and tolerably straight, with only three or four gentle curves. The terminus was actually a few yards inside the Haslingden boundary. Manchester Road was the 'posh' part of Accrington, there being a number of large imposing houses, also the Oakhill and Haworth Parks.

In steam days the line was something of a nightmare to work; especially in wet weather. The engines sometimes ran out of steam on the long climb, then it was a case of *all hand to the pumps* — the passengers had to get out and push. There were also some hair-raising descents, when the weight overpowered the brakes, and the crew fought desperately for control, but there were no serious calamities.

Wired up

When electrification began in 1907, Haslingden had not fully decided to electrify their section of the route; in any case, the lease had still a few more months to run. However, Haslingden agreed to pay for the electrification, but were quite content to let Accrington work the line, as before. As far as the centre of Haslingden, the line was opened on 21st September 1908, and through to Lockgate a month later. In the meantime Accrington transferred four steam cars to the small depot in Haslingden to maintain a service through the town until electrification was completed. The four steam cars were then worked back to Accrington and scrapped.

The new outward track for the Baxenden section from Peel Street along Abbey Street to Blackburn Road was laid in, and from this latter point the track was double all the way to Oakhill Park gates. At Wesley Methodist Church a slight left-hand bend in the road denoted a change of name – from Abbey Street to Manchester Road. From Oakhill Park to the terminus the line was single, with passing loops at Harcourt Road, Baxenden Mission, St. John's Church, Alliance Street, and Baxenden Station. From here the track belonged to Haslingden Corporation, beginning with a short length of single line, then an elongated loop round the bend by Holland's Pie Factory, single again to the centre of Haslingden. Passing loops were at Rising Bridge, Acre, and Hud Hey. From this point the road became narrower and more tortuous, being built up on both sides with terraced housing. Approaching Haslingden centre the line doubled, and remained so through the centre of the town, the rest being single to Lockgate, with loops at Rifle Street and the Rose and Crown. At Road End the line turned sharply left on a short length of double track, and reached the boundary at Lockgate. This was a cheerless, open, windswept spot, with nothing in sight but two houses, and the buildings of the Rossendale General Hospital on the hillside above. Hardly anyone ever got on or off a tram at Lockgate unless the car was not going any further. From Lockgate to Queen's Square, Rawtenstall, the line was single, with one passing loop halfway, and double track through the centre of the town.

Squabbles

There was considerable wrangling between the three Corporations with regard to operating, and the price of electric power, which took some time to settle amicably. Accrington, backed by Haslingden, proposed that a joint service of Accrington and Rawtenstall cars should work through between Accrington and Bacup. Rawtenstall did not care for this for some reason, but eventually agreed to it for a trial period of twelve months, from 1st April 1910, renewable if the parties were agreeable, for a year at a time. The service proved quite successful, and continued until 31st December 1916, when Rawtenstall withdrew from the agreement owing to wartime conditions. From then the service worked only between Accrington and Rawtenstall, the through running to Bacup never being restored.

Half a Farthing

Accrington and Haslingden were agreed on the charge for electricity, at $1^1/_2$ pence per unit, but Rawtenstall demanded more — $1^3/_4$d — on the grounds that Accrington cars consumed more current than theirs, Rawtenstall's cars were fitted with the Raworth regenerative braking system, which was supposed to save up to 25% of current used, the Accrington cars, being fitted with the normal system of control, would consume more current, and therefore Accrington should pay more. Accrington's reply to this statement was that in their opinion Rawtenstall cars had not enough power to climb the long rise from Accrington to Baxenden without using more current than they claimed.

To settle this argument it was agreed that one car of each authority should be loaded with sandbags to the equivalent weight of a full load of passengers, and travel the entire route from Accrington to Bacup, in both directions, and at the end, to compare the amount of current used, and the time taken, including a stop and restart at every alternate request stop on the journey. This was duly carried out; Haslingden Corporation officials acting as neutral observers, and the results compared. To everyone's surprise, the difference between the Accrington and Rawtenstall cars was just over one per cent – in favour of Rawtenstall. It was agreed that this difference was not worth bothering about, and so the matter was settled amicably, a price of $1^5/_8$ pence per unit being agreed upon.

The End of the Lines

In May 1929 Rawtenstall announced that they were preparing to abandon their electric tramways. At a joint meeting of the three authorities concerned on the 15th July it was agreed to close the Accrington-Rawtenstall tramway as from 31st March 1930. A conference three weeks later at Haslingden settled most of the details of the jointly-operated bus services which would replace the trams. This was the beginning of the end for Accrington, as in one fell swoop they were destined to lose half their system. It was patently not economic to carry on indefinitely with the remainders. The bombshell dropped by Oswaldtwistle U.D.C. shortly afterwards concerning the reconstruction of Union Road was the last straw. Faced with all this trouble and expense which had not been anticipated, Accrington reluctantly decided to close the whole of the remaining tramways as from 26th August 1931.

The Great War Years

During the First World War, everything proceeded much as usual, though the call-up of men to the forces did produce some problems. However, a number of women were enrolled as conductresses, four became drivers, and one an inspector, also a number took over the jobs of clerks and cleaners in the depot. In 1917 came a directive from the Board of Trade concerning the conservation of electric power, either by reducing services, or by the elimination of some request stops. The Corporation

No. 14 stands at the Clayton Canal Bridge terminus, with the Conservative Club on the right and the *Albion* pub on the left. Something tells us that the photo was taken either at dinner time or school chucking-out time.

In June 1928 Accrington celebrated the 50th anniversary of its Incorporation as a borough. As part of the Jubilee celebrations, the Tramways Department decorated this single-decker to tour the town. The large building which the pedestrian is looking at is the *Commercial Hotel*.

'Tank Week' was held in Accrington, Blackburn and Darwen from Monday 28 January 1918 as a way of fund-raising for the war-hit government treasury. The towns competed with each other to see which could raise the most savings. This tram disguised as a tank was part of Accrington's effort. It ran throughout the week to Blackburn, where a real tank, named 'Egbert' was on display in front of the Town Hall. Tanks were new in warfare then, and Egbert had seen action in France and Belgium. It was of a male type — there were female tanks too. Conductresses and female cleaners were only appointed in 1917 because of the shortage of male labour.

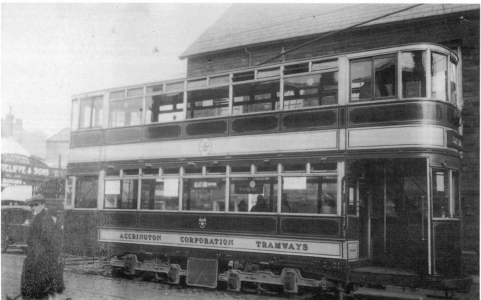

With Infant Street chapel and Seth Sutcliffe's emporium in the background, here is no. 41 about to leave for Clayton.

Photo by W. Gratwicke

deliberated on this for six months, then decided to cut out a few stops. Six stops were cut out on the Baxenden and Haslingden route, five on Oswaldtwistle, three on Clayton and one on Burnley Road. The remaining stops were adjusted so that they were more or less equidistant.

In 1916, Blackburn applied for an increase in mileage allowance for their cars working over the Accrington line from Church. However, a new agreement was negotiated, coming into force on 1st January 1917, whereby to balance the mileage, Accrington had to provide two cars to work on a joint service — hitherto the service had been worked by Blackburn alone. So Accrington had to remove the roofs from three double deck cars, so that they would pass under the 15ft 6in bridge at Blythe's Works, Church. Nos. 9, 10 and 17 were chosen for this alteration, two cars to work the service, and one spare.

Steel Saves Brass

Later in 1917 a chance came along to acquire a considerable amount of tramway rails and overhead wiring at a knockdown price. There is no indication in the minutes as to who unearthed this 'find', or where it came from. There was much more than Accrington needed so it was put to the five adjoining authorities — Accrington, Blackburn, Darwen, Haslingden and Rawtenstall — to make a joint purchase of this material, to be put into a pool, which each of the five could draw upon when necessary. The proposal was readily agreed to, and as a result each of the five saved several thousand pounds over the following years.

Harry Pilling

In July 1916 a letter was received from the Borough Treasurer of Haslingden who stated that his Council has given permission for the small tram depot at Haslingden to be used as a store for waste paper. As Accrington out-stationed four trams in the depot, the manager (Harry Pilling) was sent post haste to examine the situation. He was appalled at what he saw; loose paper and bags stacked all over the place, even between the trams, and he immediately ordered the withdrawal of the four cars from the depot, owing to the risk of fire. This entailed rescheduling of duties, since these cars would now have to work from Accrington. As it happened, there never was a fire in the Haslingden depot, but Mr Pilling was taking no chances. Mr Pilling, who was appointed Depot Superintendent in 1907, became Tramways Manager in 1910, and held this post, later designated 'Transport Manager', until his retirement in 1944. He was succeeded by George Armstrong, previously Transport Manager of Exeter City Council.

He was a strict executive, but was well liked by both staff and council officials, and when in 1918 he applied for the post of manager of a much larger tramway, the Council begged him not to go, and increased his salary – so he stayed, much to everyone's relief.

Shelter from the Stormy Blast

The most vexed question which came up time and time again during those years was concerning the lack of shelter at the Market Place for tram passengers. In wet weather there were only two possibilities — to go into the Market Hall, or try and shelter under the covers of the stalls — but these were only available on market days. The market entrances became a seething mass of humanity, customers trying to squeeze their way in and out amongst a crowd of tram passengers. Mr Pilling wanted to erect barriers to make passengers form orderly queues, but the General Works Committee would have none of this; they said it would impede the passage of the public up and down Peel Street, and would reduce the number of market stalls appreciably. There seemed no answer to this impasse until November 1919, when a gift of £150 was received from Thomas Gordon, a retired Accrington magistrate, then living in Blackpool, for the erection of a shelter at the Market Place. The Borough Engineer designed it, and the materials for its construction were provided by a local firm of engineers, Lang Bridge & Co., at cost price. The shelter was brought into use in May 1920. It was built of iron, with a lead-covered wooden roof. It was in two halves, with a covered passageway in between to give access to the Market Hall entrance. The upper half was all windows, and wooden seats were fitted round the walls inside. Three market stalls had to be sacrificed so that it could be erected adjoining the pavement. A clock was fitted under the roof, in the passageway. It was greatly appreciated by everyone, and was well used.

Born in a blaze of contention, it died in the same way. Over the years, with the rearrangement of bus termini, most of which no longer started at the Market Place, it became more or less redundant in 1945, and the Council decided to remove it. By this time it had become nothing more than a meeting place for the town's pensioners, who congregated there to discuss various topics of the day. The proposal to demolish it met with vociferous protests from the old folk. In consequence, it was allowed to stay for the time being, but the Council decided to use one half of the shelter as an office for the bus inspectors. At this the old folk adopted an 'all or nothing' attitude, with the result that the Council lost patience, and in 1953, ordered that it be demolished.

The Electric Cars

The four single deck and fourteen double-deck cars delivered to Accrington in 1907 were standard designs of the Brush Company. The single deckers, numbered 1 to 4, had open platforms and a saloon divided into three parts by internal partitions with sliding doors. The short end sections, which seated eight passengers in each, were intended for smokers, but after a short time in service, the partitions had proved to be rather a nuisance, as they restricted the easy movement of passengers. Consequently, when two further cars of the type were ordered in 1908, the partitions were omitted, and in the next two years, the partitions in nos. 1 to 4 were removed, the two drop windows in each end section being taken out and

Here we see no. 21 passing the Town Hall on its way to the railway viaduct. The corner of Dutton Street is seen on the right, at the shop where Accringtonians bought their Steinway pianos. The horse seems to be making heavy weather of pulling that cart.

replaced by a single fixed window. Two other cars, nos. 23 (ordered in 1909) and 27 (obtained two years later) were of the same pattern, without partitions. No more cars of this type were ordered, the total remaining at eight. They had four fixed windows each side, without top lights, ventilation being by means of the clerestory type roof. These cars were used principally on the Burnley Road – Oswaldtwistle service. They rarely ventured anywhere else, and never reached either Rawtenstall or Blackburn. No. 6, of this class, had the honour of being the very last tram to run in Accrington.

Jumbos

The fourteen double deck cars were considerably larger. Their upper decks were fitted with four drop-framed windows each side, the lower deck having three fixed windows with pairs of opening top-lights over them. Their platforms and the end balconies of the upper deck were open. They seated 22 passengers on longitudinal seats down below, and eighteen in the upper saloon, on seats for two on one side of the gangway, and for one on the other side. On each balcony was a curved seat for five, giving a total of 50 altogether. These cars were numbered 5 to 18 originally, but on the delivery of the two extra single deckers in 1908, nos. 5 and 6 were renumbered 19 and 20, to make way for them. Extra cars of this type were added in 1909 (nos. 21, 22); 1910 (nos. 24, 25) and 1912 (no. 26) making a total of 19 of this class.

All these cars, nos. 1 to 26, were fitted with four wheeled radial trucks, built on the Conaty & Lycett patent, by the Brush company, with a wheelbase of 8ft 6in. By 1912 some trouble had developed with these trucks through uneven wear in the bearings, leading to jerky movements and strange noises. The Brush company was consulted, and they sent a radial truck of their own design for trial; this was put under car no. 12, and tested for three weeks, but was not satisfactory. Eventually an arrangement was made with Brush, for the trucks to be returned to Loughborough two at a time, for modification, in which the radial gear would be removed, and the axleboxes given a slight amount of extra side play. The first two tracks were dealt with in 1913, and proved very good on trial, but unfortunately with the outbreak of war, the process was severely interfered with, and the last of the 27 trucks was not dealt with until 1919.

Jumbos Plus

In 1914 it was decided to order some larger cars, especially to cope with the weekends and peak periods. The Brush Co. were asked to submit designs for single and double deck cars, with eight wheels instead of four. Two types were chosen, and an order for three single deck and two double deck cars was made. However, owing to the outbreak of war, and the restrictions put on the car builders by the War Office, these cars were not delivered until 1919. After a trial period, a further order for two more single-deck and two double-deck cars was placed late in 1919, and these were delivered in 1920. The five single-deck cars were numbered 28 to 32, and the four double-deck 38 to 41, the gap of five in the numbering being left in anticipation of further single deckers being ordered in the future.

All these cars were all-enclosed, having windows round the platforms, and in the case of the double deckers, enclosed balconies on the upper deck. The single-deck cars had five windows each side, without opening top lights, and a clerestory roof, whilst the double-deck variety also had five side windows, but with pairs of opening top lights in each deck. Seating in both cases was longitudinal in the lower deck, for 40 in the single-decker and 32 in the double-deck cars. The latter had 2+1 seating upstairs, with a curved seat for 7 on each balcony, a total of 76. They were fitted with Brush LCC maximum traction trucks of 4ft 6in wheelbase.

Once again I digress to explain a technicality. Maximum traction trucks were only fitted to eight-wheeled trams, one truck at each end of the body. In these, the two pairs of wheels in each truck were of different diameters; the larger pair, which were driven by the motor, were usually 32in diameter, and the smaller pair 22in. The pivot by which the truck was attached to the body was not in the centre of the truck (as was the case with railway carriages for instance) but was arranged as near as possible to the axle driven by the motor. By this means, most of the dead weight of the tram was carried by the driven axle, giving better adhesion to the rails.

The LCC truck was designed by the Brush Co. in consultation with the London County Council Tramways (hence the designation LCC) who wanted a stronger and neater design than the others currently available, the Brush BB type and the Brill 22E, both of which were ugly pieces of machinery, though satisfactory in performance. The LCC truck was a neat design, devoid of projecting springs and other pieces, but it could not be put into full production owing to war conditions, so did not get going until 1919 or 1920. The LCC purchased several hundreds of them, and they became popular with other operators. The Accrington cars were originally intended to have Brill 22E trucks (an American design, but built in England) but by mutual consent they were delivered in 1920/21 with the new LCC trucks, and proved very satisfactory cars.

These large cars came into service mainly at weekends, but also occasionally on other days at peak periods. The single-deckers worked mainly on the Burnley Road – Oswaldtwistle service, but sometimes ran elsewhere, including Clayton and even Blackburn, but they never went beyond Baxenden on the Rawtenstall route. The double-deck cars were confined to the Clayton-Church run; though for football matches they did appear on Burnley Road occasionally.

Still they come — Ossie Rejoices

Finally, in 1926 the Corporation bought two Brush low-floor double-deck cars, nos. 42 and 43, which were almost identical in appearance to the large cars (38-41) but had Peckham P22 four wheeled trucks, with roller bearing axleboxes. These cars had their lower deck floors under the main frames, as opposed to normal double- deckers, which had the floor on top of the frames. By this means, and also a slight reduction in head-room on both decks, the overall height was reduced to 14ft 6in, which meant that they could pass under the low railway bridge at Church station with three inches to spare. They were hailed with enthusiasm by the people of Oswaldtwistle, and they worked this route almost exclusively. One was tried on the Blackburn run, and since they could negotiate the bridge at Blythe's works, Church, with ease, latterly one was working the Oswaldtwistle route, while the other worked to Blackburn. No doubt, had the tram system not been doomed to extinction, more of these cars would have been purchased to replace the 1907 cars. They had four windows with top lights on each side, seating 26 in the lower deck and 34 upstairs.

Alterations

During their life of almost 25 years, some alterations were made to the older double-decker cars. Firstly, in 1917, nos. 9, 10 and 17 had their upper deck roofs and windows removed, making them open-topped, for the new joint service to Blackburn. Their top covers were stored in the depot for possible future use. Next, in 1919, no. 13 was experimentally fitted with windows round the platforms, which was a great improvement in that it gave the platform staff almost complete protection from rain and wind. This was approved by all concerned, and it was resolved to similarly alter all the rest of the cars as opportunity permitted. At the closure of the system only six double-deck cars remained with open platforms, nos. 7, 14, 17, 20, 25 and 26. The two open topped cars, 9 and 10, received enclosed platforms in 1920, but the third, no. 17, which was regarded as a spare, was never done, and indeed became the first car of the fleet to be scrapped, in December 1929.

Finally, in March 1924, no. 11 was taken into the works and drastically altered. Blackburn had been experimenting for some time with covered top decks for their fleet, but the varying heights of railway bridges on their system was a problem. The lowest — at Church — had a headroom of 15ft 6in, and they found that by fitting wheels six inches smaller (26" diameter) than normal, and reducing the headroom in the upper deck, they could produce a top-covered car which would just scrape under the bridge. Mr Pilling decided to do something of the same sort with his cars, and accordingly no. 11 became the guinea pig. The car was taken to pieces; the lower deck upright pillars were shortened by $7^1/_2$ inches and those of the upper deck by $3^1/_2$ inches. By fitting 26in wheels, with high speed motors, he produced a car only 15ft 1in high. The platforms were enclosed at the same time. After trials, a second car, no. 24, was altered in the same way in June 1924.

Accrington now had two covered-top cars which could work the Blackburn service. The open-toppers, 9 and 10, now being redundant, had their covered tops restored. There was one snag, however. No. 11 had the earlier top deck with four drop-framed windows, and reducing the height proved no problem, but no. 24 had the later type with three fixed windows with opening top lights, and reducing the height of these produced problems. So, though no. 9 got its original top cover back, that of no. 10 had to be used for no. 24, so they exchanged top covers, no. 10 receiving the three-windowed one.

Spick and Span

Maintenance was always of a very high order. The cars were well cleaned and free from squeaks and rattles which speak of bodies coming apart at the seams, and the jolts and bangs which denote lack of attention to the running gear. Not until late in 1930 did one ever see a car which was not spick and span. From this point in time, it was obviously not economic to do a lot of work on the trams, and by May 1931, nos. 7, 14 and 20 were in a truly disreputable state, and were withdrawn. Single deck car no. 4 spent several months with an unpainted length of plywood nailed to one of its lower panels, and no. 6 made history as the last car in service — but with a prodigious dent in one dashplate, which it had had for some time.

The livery was bright red and cream, lined out in gold on red panels, and brown on cream. Roofs were a bright orange brown,

Seen in Peel Street with the Market Hall and the Gordon shelter as background, No. 9 is about to set off for Blackburn. This tram was altered to an open-top car for the Blackburn service in 1917 and fitted with an enclosed platform in 1920. Late in 1924 it was refitted with its original roofed upper deck.

Photo by W. Gratwicke

and frames and running gear maroon. The full legend ACCRINGTON CORPORATION TRAMWAYS was carried in gold letters, shaded blue, on the bottom side panels, the large numerals being also in gold with blue shadings, in the centre of each dashplate. Slight variations occurred from time to time, some double-deck cars having both upper deck side panels cream, while others had the upper panel red. In 1918, Mr Pilling completely banned the external advertisements which had disgraced the cars up to then, and from 1919 onwards there could be no smarter looking trams anywhere.

'Standards' (or 'Poles')
For Supporting Overhead Wires

Accrington used two types; the bracket arm, used on normal width roads, and the span wire type, for wider roads, the object being to bring the power wires as near the centre of the road as possible. Bracket arms could be of different lengths, according to the needs of the location. Tapered iron tubes were used for the poles, embedded in concrete and sunk from 4 to 6 feet into the ground, as necessitated by the conditions. Those carrying the wires round bends were subject to slightly greater stresses than on straight sections, and the dead weight of the bracket arms had also to be allowed for. Conversely, the span wire type were subject to less stress, since two poles were used, on opposite sides of the road, with the open wire stretched between them. Often the bracket arm carried a lamp about half way along, to give some additional lighting to the roadway. A certain amount of wrought iron ornamental scroll-work was applied to the poles, not very much in Accrington's case, but some tramways used to go a bit over the top in this respect. The power wires were slung from brackets near the end of the arm, or from the span wire. In either case, adequate ceramic insulators were fitted at the joints to prevent leakage of current into the ironwork, which would have been dangerous to the public. The power wires were usually fitted at a height of 20 feet above ground level, except under bridges, where special arrangements might be necessary. The wiring was divided into half mile sections by a short gap, and at these points a 'feeder' box was placed at the roadside, with a cable running up the pole to the overhead power wires, to maintain the current at the correct voltage. Drivers were instructed to shut off current when passing these feeder points to obviate a short-circuit

Some Tramway Characters
Driver Holland's is rather an interesting story. Sometime in the 1890's, a Dutchman named Jan van der Sluys came over to England and settled in Accrington. He obtained a job as a carpenter in the steam tram depot, married a local girl, and they had a son, Willem. His workmates had considerable difficulty with his name, and consequently usually referred to him as 'the Hollander'. So in 1909 he changed his name by deed poll to John Holland, and his son became William.

When he was fourteen, William got a job in the tramway depot, and worked his way up to a driver (or motorman, to give it the official title). William was popular with his workmates, and it was a tragedy that he had the accident at Clayton which incapacitated him for several months, but he was able to hold down a job in the depot.

Another character, whose proper name I never knew, was an elderly driver who sported a long white beard, which reached down to his waist. It was always beautifully kept, and he was proud of it. When driving, he draped his beard over the front of the dashplate, and it was a never-ending source of wonder how he managed to manipulate the controls without getting his beard tangled up in them — but he never did. He retired about 1926, before the threat of closure came into being. He was known to all and sundry as 'The Mayor of Laneside' — for some reason not explained.

The third member of this little coterie was one of the 'once seen, never forgotten' brigade. He was a very small individual, about 5ft 4in in height, and was a conductor on the trams and buses for many years. At first sight, one was convinced that one of the Brooke Bond chimpanzees had been pressed into service; a more monkey-like little man it is difficult to imagine. Despite his simian appearance, he was a cheerful little chap, who never took offence at the remarks made about him, and of course, was well known and well liked by the passengers.

I was once put in a very embarrassing position when out one afternoon with my family. We were on a bus — and this little fellow was the conductor. I had seen our elder daughter (then aged seven) staring at the conductor with a look of disbelief on her face, and suddenly, at a stop when everything was quiet, she piped up with *'Mum, doesn't that man look like a monkey?'* The bus exploded in laughter, but our little ape-man never turned a hair, he just joined in the laughter. For my part, I wished that I could have crawled under the seats. When we got off, at the terminus, I apologised to him for my daughter's terrible faux pas, but he just grinned and said *'Think nothing of it, sir, it happens all the time. I'm used to it, and it doesn't affect me in the least'.* A great little character, who we were sorry to lose when he retired.

The last of this group was 'Jock' Murdoch, whose life was so tragically cut short by the crash at Rising Bridge in 1930. He was a

One of the new electric trams, no.18, at Oakleigh, Whalley Road.

services were with the Accrington & District Sunday School Union, who presented him in 1945 with a diploma commemorating his 50 years unbroken services to Wesley Methodist Church and Sunday School. In the mid 1930s he was also secretary of the very successful Sunday School Union Eisteddfod, an annual event which included a musical and literary festival, also an arts and crafts exhibition. The large number of floral tributes at his funeral in 1953 confirmed the high esteem in which he was held by all who knew him.

quiet, even tempered and unflappable Scot, who spoke little, though his Scottish accent endeared him to most people. Being over six feet tall, he caused the depot clerks some trouble, since there were certain cars he could not drive in comfort, owing to his height, and they had to be careful which cars they assigned to him on his duties. He was courteous and helpful, endearing himself to staff and passengers alike, and his untimely end shocked a great many people. He was sorely missed.

A Real Gent

Another notable character was Charles Albert Gent, who lived in Moorhouse Avenue, Accrington for many years. He had the proud record of never once being late for work, or for an appointment in his voluntary services in other directions, during the entire 30 years he worked for the Transport Department. He was accorded the honour of driving the last electric tram to work the Baxenden service 30th March 1930. Mr Gent was not a regular driver, being called upon for relief duties and workmen's services in the rush hours. He retired from the Transport Department in 1939, in his time having just seen the last of the steam trams, then working with the electric cars, and finally the buses. His service began in 1909 in the paint shop in Ellison Street depot, then working his way up the ladder to be appointed foreman of the bus cleaning gang, a position he held for ten years. On a voluntary basis, he was secretary of the depot Sick Club for 16 years. His chief voluntary

It is admitted that these two trams are from the Blackburn, not Accrington, fleet. They are passing near to Blythe's sidings, on the Blackburn side of Church terminus. This action shot of a chap sweeping up what was sometimes called 'coddy muck' was probably taken by Mr Harrison, an Accrington professional photographer, just a few years after 1901, when the line was electrified.

The driver of this tram is posing for this (c.1910?) photo, for he is at the wrong end of the tram. The conductor, seen wearing his ticket machine strapped over his left shoulder, has already turned the trolley around for the trip back to Accrington from the Clayton canal bridge terminus. The other official, wearing his uniform greatcoat, is probably the tram inspector. The postman stepping off the tram is concentrating on his bag of mail, oblivious to our cameraman.

BLACKBURN ROAD, ACCRINGTON.

In the early 1930s, bus no. 83 is passing the market stalls, on its way to Baxenden. There's still evidence of the tramtracks but the overhead wires have gone. In the distance a double-decker is seen, as well as a single-decker at the stop between Dutton Street and St James Street. Note the presence of traffic lights at the junction of Blackburn Road with Church Street. On the far side of this junction a few years later (1937?) a pillar was erected to allow for telephone communications between the police station and the policeman on his town centre beat. By opening a door on the metal pillar, members of the public could speak to the police station. A switch operated in the station made the orange light on top of the pillar flash to attract the bobby's attention.

No. 113, one of the Leyland PD2 1947 batch, is on a workmen's service, as denoted by the 'W' in the route number box. It is standing in Cannon Street, near the junction with St James' Street, which was not part of a regular bus route, so it may have just been 'parked' while awaiting its departure time. Behind the bus is a sign which gives the impression that the pupils of St James' School were dangerous.

THE ADVENT OF BUSES

Accrington Corporation was rather slow in anticipating the rise of the motor bus, and did not apply for powers to operate them until 1927, in anticipation of the 50th anniversary (in 1928) of the incorporation of the town as a borough. Also applied for at the same time were powers to incorporate the adjoining Urban Districts of Church, Oswaldtwistle and Clayton, also the Parish of Huncoat, into the borough, with County Borough status. However, though the bus powers were granted by Parliament; the extension of the borough was not — all they were allowed was the Parish of Huncoat. Not until 1974, with the general shake-up of municipalities ordered by the government was anything in this respect achieved. The Borough of Hyndburn was formed by the amalgamation of Accrington, Church, Oswaldtwistle, Clayton, Great Harwood, Rishton and Altham. Altham had been part of Burnley Rural District.

In the Beginning

Motor buses began to get a foothold in Accrington in 1922, when Ribble Motor Services inaugurated a service to Burnley. They were followed by Kenyon, Coleman and Robinson (K.C.R.) of Blackburn with services to Padiham, Great Harwood, and Rishton in 1923. These were closely followed by the Rishton and Antley Motor Co., who began similar services to Great Harwood and Rishton, also one completely within the borough:- up Ormerod Street to Willows Lane and Green Haworth. Lakeland & Pickup, also Moore's (of Great Harwood) began a service via Great Harwood and Whalley to Clitheroe. (Moore's later became the Calder Motor Co.) L. & P. went out of business in 1924, when two of their three char-a-bancs were wrecked in a collision on Sandy Brow, the stiff rise out of Whalley. All the others were absorbed by Ribble between 1927 and 1930. Consequently when Accrington obtained their bus powers — to operate anywhere within a five-mile radius of the Town Hall — most of the available routes were already taken up.

The first Corporation routes were opened in November 1928, between the Market Place and Huncoat station, and to Higher Antley and Woodnook. Six buses were purchased, all on Dennis chassis, with bodies by the Brush Co. Two of these, on Dennis G type chassis, were 18-seaters, numbered 44 and 45, the other four were on E type chassis with 32 seater bodies, nos 50-53. On 3 December 1928 a through limited stop service was arranged with Haslingden and Rawtenstall (both of whom had operated buses for several years) between Accrington and Bacup, jointly operated by the three. Though running in parallel with the trams, the latter did not suffer much since most of the tramway traffic was short distance. A similar joint express service was begun in 1929 between Accrington and Blackburn. In 1930, Accrington contributed £2250 towards the purchase by Ribble of the Rishton & Antley Motor Co., thereby gaining a half share in certain Ribble services – Green Haworth, Accrington – Whalley – Clitheroe, Oswaldtwistle – Clayton – Gt. Harwood – Clitheroe, and Accrington – Burnley. Relations with Ribble were always very good, and the two concerns worked amicably together for many years.

Four more Dennis E buses (nos. 54-57) were obtained in 1929, plus two 48 seat double-deckers (nos. 58,59) on Dennis H type chassis, with Brush patent low-height bodies. These were solidly built, and were rather heavy, rendering them sluggish in operations. The 24 upstairs seats were single bucket-type, arranged herringbone fashion down the centre, with a gangway at each side. Only two drivers on the staff really mastered these two monsters, and could make them move; for the most part they worked on the Blackburn and Burnley services, where there were not many stops. It is hardly surprising that these were the first two buses to be sold – to the military authorities for service in Lincolnshire, in 1940. The coming of four 32 seater Dennis EV buses in 1930 (nos.

46-49) saw the last purchases of this make for many years, also the last Brush bodies.

On their Own

When the tramways closed in 1930 and 1931, considerable additions had to be made to the bus fleet, and for a considerable time they were all Leylands, with mostly Leyland bodies. Six LT's with 32 seat bodies, (Nos 60-65) began to work the Rawtenstall service in 1930, and were followed by several batches of TD1 double deckers with 52 or 54 seater bodies (Nos 66-87). After these there was a gap until 1937, when eight TD5s were added, with 56-seater bodies (Nos 88-95). Four Leyland Tigers (TS1) (Nos 40-43) were purchased in 1932, with 32 seater bodies, and a further four (Nos 36-39) on TS8 chassis in 1938. From then it was decided that single deck buses should take the lowest numbers, from 1 upwards, and double deck continue the higher numbering. (LT1, TD1, TD5, etc. are the codes by which the manufacturers classed the differing types of chassis).

In addition to replacing the tramways, other services were established to various parts of the town — to the housing estates of Laneside, Fern Gore, Spring Hill, Woodnook and Within Grove (Huncoat) — also via Charter Street to Moscow Mill, and via Countess Street to Church Kirk, and there were several purely workmen's services to and from the larger workshops in the area, as well as special services for schools.

Livery Reflects Pride

Some interesting details have come to light recently, concerning the colours in which the Accrington buses were painted. The electric trams were bright red and pale cream, with orange-brown roofs, and it was expected that the new buses, when they came along in 1928, would be the same. To everyone's surprise, they were entirely different. There is no mention of this in the Transport Committee minutes. Some people had expressed the view that a change of colour might be desirable, since most of the buses operating into Accrington were various shades of red or maroon — Ribble, Rishton & Antley, Calder, Claremont, and Rawtenstall Corporation. Only Haslingden and Blackburn Corporations were different.

When the first buses appeared on the streets in November 1928, they were a great surprise in their dark blue with two red stripes; they were unusual, very smart, and were favourably commented upon. The ever-growing fleet became well known throughout a good deal of the county. A casual conversation in the local library only a few weeks ago produced the information that the colours of the East Lancashire Regiment were dark blue, maroon and cream. The 'Accrington Pals' formed a part of this Regiment in the First World War, and their tragic fate at the Battle of the Somme in 1916 is a significant part of Accrington's history. Was this the reason for the choice of blue and red for Accrington's buses? It might well be, though still there has been no official confirmation of this theory, which is enhanced by the painting of the bus window frames black instead of cream. It is suggested that this is as a commemoration of the 'Accrington Pals' awful fate.

Whether this was the true reason for the choice of the bus colours, and who suggested it, we shall probably never know for certain, but it is too much of a coincidence to assume that the colours were chosen by accident. If this is the truth of the matter, it is a great pity that it was not made known years ago, the people of Accrington would have appreciated it greatly. Sadly, coincidence or not, the colours of the local buses are now lost for ever, with the demise of Hyndburn Transport in 1997.

Still, this mobile tribute to the 'Accrington Pals' was in existence for almost seventy years, which is something to be grateful for.

War Time

The outbreak of war in 1939 presented many problems. Services had to be reduced, both to save fuel and to release buses for essential war work, the main one in this area being to the Royal Ordnance Factory at Lower Darwen. Buses of every operator in the area could be seen there every night and morning, from as far away as Todmorden. The other factories, all on war work, had to be supplied with workers, and at times every bus in the fleet which was capable of movement was in service somewhere. The complete 'blackout' which was strictly enforced at night made things even more difficult. All motor vehicle headlamps had to be fitted with special masks which only allowed a narrow flat beam of light — just enough to

A Leyland PLSC3 bus of the 'Rishton & Calder' company, outside Accrington Grammar School in the late 1920s, bound for Gt. Harwood. The Rishton & Antley company combined with the Calder Motor Co. (formerly Moore's) of Gt. Harwood, and ran for a time labelled 'Rishton & Calder', but very shortly afterwards, in 1930, was absorbed by Ribble Motors. This bus was originally one of the Calder fleet. At this time, the Grammar School had pupils of both sexes.

Undoubtedly one of the earliest photos of a bus which transported folk along Accrington's roads, this is a Crossley, Regd no. TC 5456, first registered by Lancashire County Council Motor Taxation Office in 1923 for the Rishton & Antley (R & A) Motor Company, no. 14 in their fleet. It was sold to Ribble Motors when Ribble acquired R & A in 1930. The destination board reads 'Church and Dill Hall'.

One of the four Burlingham-bodied Leyland buses, no. 1, at the bottom of Ellison Street — the gable-end of the 'new' depot can be seen top left. The bus has been repainted in the standard blue and red livery. As delivered, and for about four years, they were painted green and cream as an experiment. The design of the body was such that the red stripe below the windows was very narrow, and is hardly discernible. The repainting dates the photo at about 1952. The front doors of The Hippodrome theatre are visible.

A view inside the bus depot in Ellison Street, in 1937. Leyland TD5 bus no. 88, with Leyland-built body has apparently just been delivered. The Leyland chassis to the right is not identifiable, neither are the other three buses on the extreme right. The chassis is a bit of a mystery, being without a body. Perhaps the body has been removed completely for some purpose. At this period, and for a few years before and after, all the buses had Leyland-built bodies, so a chassis on its own from the Leyland works seems unlikely. The fact that it has no registration plate heightens the mystery.

see where one was going — and buses were allowed one blue lamp in each deck, giving a minimum of light. If an air raid warning was sounded, buses had to stop wherever they were, and disgorge their passengers, and they were not allowed to move again until the 'all clear' was sounded. Street lighting was reduced to an absolute minimum, and pedestrians were allowed to carry a small pencil torch, which must always be directed onto the ground. During the hours of darkness, one moved almost at one's peril.

In November 1942, in view of wartime conditions, a number of cuts were made to services, and it was ordained that the last buses on week days should run at 9.30 p.m., and on Saturdays, 10 p.m. A week later, some adjustments were made in the light of what had been experienced in that short period. On 1st April 1943 a curfew was imposed: after 7.00 p.m. only workmen's services were operated. Full normal services were reinstated from 3rd October 1945, the war having ended completely two months earlier, and though supplies were still somewhat restricted, general regulations had been considerably relieved.

The Corporation goes Commercial

On 5th September 1949, after a rather stormy meeting, the Transport Committee passed a resolution that advertisements should be allowed on the outside of buses, and some were applied almost immediately. In a subsequent meeting on 8th April 1950, the advertisements were vigorously attacked by Cllr. Constantine as being 'hideous', but his protests had no effect. Some time later, in March 1959, in spite of great protests from church leaders and some of the Councillors, it was agreed to allow advertisements for alcoholic drink to be shown on the buses.

The application of advertisements to the outside panels of buses certainly added to the revenue, but their general effect was not popular — in Cllr. Constantine's words, they were a disgrace, but they continued until the de-regulation in 1985. Most of the public did not like them, and took little notice of them. Mr Pilling had banned advertisements on the trams in 1919, and the result of this was that the vehicles — both trams and buses — looked very smart and well kept. The return to advertisements in 1949 was certainly a retrograde step in this context.

New Stock

In wartime, only two motor manufacturers, Guy and Daimler, were allowed to build bus chassis, and these only in restricted numbers. Only 'utility' bodies were allowed to be fitted, with plain wooden seats, no interior panelling, and of very angular design, very little curved panelling being allowed. To obtain a new bus, operators had to go through a very strict examination by the authorities as to why it was required. Only 56 seater bodies were made. If circumstances compelled the use of a single-deck bus, then only the Bedford OB chassis was available, with a similar 32 seat 'utility' body. Accrington managed to acquire nine of these Guy double deckers, but not until 1944 to 1946, when restrictions were slightly eased. Four of these (nos. 44, 45, 58 and 59) were regarded as replacements, the other five (nos 96-100) being additions to the fleet. These utility buses gave yeoman service, and were instrumental in the Corporation purchasing a number of Guy buses after the war. In fact, from 1946 to 1971, nine Guy single-deck and 28 double-deck buses were bought, along with 19 Leyland single and 37 double-decks. From 1972 onwards, 29 Leyland Atlanteans were added to stock, bringing the fleet numbers up to 199. No. 195 was an oddment — a Dennis version of the Atlantean — and subsequently a further eight of these were purchased, in pairs, between 1981 and 1985 — the last new buses purchased by the Corporation. (nos 101-108).

Some oddments were also bought. For example, four Daimler CVD6 chassis with 56-seater Roberts bodies, (nos 123-126) these being part of a cancelled order for Colchester Corporation. They were not popular with the drivers owing to their fluid-flywheels and semi-automatic gear boxes, but they lasted for 14 years. Thirteen Bristol RESL/6L single-deckers, and five Seddon RU's were obtained for comparison purposes in 1968 to 1976 (nos 25–42). No 38 of the Seddon batch was fitted with a 39-seat coach body, for private hire work. From this period almost all bodies were built by the East Lancashire Coachbuilders Co. of Blackburn. The Leyland single-deckers obtained over the post-war period were either 'Leopards' or 'Panthers'. The nine Guy single-deck buses were six 'Arab 3's' (5-10) and three LUF (14-16) — (Leyland engine

A line-up on Ellison's tenement alongside the depot in 1946, of most of the stock of Guy Arab wartime utility buses. From left to right they are nos. 98, 97, 96, 58, 45, 44 and 99. Two are missing – nos. 59 and 100 – possibly the photographer's camera could not take in any more. Some very minor differences can be seen, due to the different body builders, chiefly the shape of the roof, and the windscreen framing, otherwise they are identical, and conform to the specifications laid down by the wartime Government.

These two Guy Wulfurians, discussed in the text of the book, are seen (36 VTF) in Peel Street and (35 VTF) passing the Town Hall. The photos were probably taken just after the pair were bought in 1961.

fitted under the floor). Of these no 10 had by far the longest career, not being disposed of until 1983, having spent the last twenty years as a breakdown and towing vehicle; all the rest had gone by 1965.

Nos 1-4 were Leyland PS1s with Burlington 35 seater-bodies, delivered in 1948, and were painted in an experimental livery of bright green and cream, contrasting starkly with the standard dark blue with two red stripes and black window frames. The experiment was not repeated, and these four were soon repainted in the standard colours. Another painting experiment was carried out in 1962, when Guy double decker no. 138 appeared with its window frames in red, instead of black. The whole effect was startling and garish; within three months the black window frames were restored.

Rolling Stock
Two other experimental buses which must be mentioned were Guy Wulfrunian double-deckers with 66-seater East Lancs bodies and rear entrances (nos 156 and 157), delivered in May 1961. They are believed to be the only Wulfrunians ever built with rear entrances. Delivery was considerably delayed, due to three-cornered consultations between Guy Motors, East Lancs Coachbuilders and Accrington Corporation, over various details. The main cause of contention was the air suspension on these vehicles. The main complaint from both passengers and staff was their tendency to roll in motion, especially when lightly loaded. One conductor told me he felt seasick, he hated the things. Anyway, they were not popular, and a great sigh of relief was heard when after only seven years they were sold to Bury Corporation, who had a few other Wulfrunians (with front entrance bodies)

Progress (?)
Something must be said about the de-regulation of buses. In 1985 the Prime Minister, Mrs Thatcher, introduced the De-regulation of Buses Act, which has resulted in the present, near-chaotic state of bus services. The main purpose of this Act was to get rid of the monopoly of the Government-owned National Bus Company, which owned around three quarters of the companies operating throughout the country – our own Ribble Motor Services was one of them. Municipal authorities such as Accrington and Blackburn

Corporations were barred by this Act from operating their own buses. The fleet and the services, had to be sold off to a private company. The Corporation however were not debarred from having a stake in these companies. They could have shares in them, but not a monopoly.

Final Straw
The final straw for Hyndburn came in 1997, when they were persuaded to sell out the entire operation to Stagecoach, at a knock-down price. This did not include the depot — for reasons best known to the Council — which makes it very awkward for Stagecoach, who have to operate the Accrington services from their depot in Blackburn. The old publicly-owned monopoly of the National Bus Co. has now been replaced by a privately owned monopoly, Stagecoach, who own almost all of the former NBC companies. The change-over has not been for the better, taken all round.

There seems no way out of this situation, which has put bus services right back to the 1920s. It was only the Road Traffic Act of 1934 which set up the Regional Traffic Commissioners to bring chaos into harmony. The only way seems to be that of restoring the complete powers of the Commissioners, and giving them the teeth to bite hard where necessary, but I don't see that happening. Maybe the Local Authorities could be given back their bus operating powers, but even given the chance, I can't see many of them taking it up, it will cost far too much.

Accrington Corporation Transport Dept.—Chief office: General Offices, Market Hall, Accrington. Gen. man., Harry Pilling, A.M.I.E.E. Ald. G. H. Ellis, J.P. (vice-chairman and Mayor), Coun. J. Lord (chairman), Alds. Sir Thomas Higham, Lambert, Couns. Bolton, Hargreaves, Harling, Kilshaw, Lancaster, Mills, O'Connor, Potts, Roberts, Slack, Smith, Tetlow. Chief clerk, S. E. Ogden; town clerk, W. H. Warhurst, LL.B. Operating motor buses only. Rolling stock: 48 (of which 8 are fitted with c.i. engines), comprising 24 four-wheel double-deck, and 24 four-wheel single-deck buses. Chassis supplied by Dennis, and Leyland; bodies by Brush, and Leyland. Route mileage, 62.

An official photograph, taken in the Brush Electrical Co's works at Loughborough, of one of the two 18-seater Dennis buses ordered for the beginning of the bus services in 1928. It was a mistake ordering these small vehicles, as they soon proved inadequate for the services required of them, and from about 1934/5 they were retained mainly for private hire work. With the out-break of war in 1939, they were soon taken out of regular use, no.44 being converted to a mobile canteen for the employees in 1940, and no. 45 became a staff vehicle, going out to pick up the operating staff from their homes in the early hours, and returning them around midnight. No. 45 was withdrawn in 1946, but no. 44 lasted until 1950.

No.1 stands near the 'Black Dog' terminus in 1948, when four new Leyland buses were experimentally painted in green and cream livery.

ACCIDENTS

Taken all round, the tramways of Accrington, both steam and electric, were remarkably free of serious accidents. They had the distinction of never having killed a passenger, though there were a number of injuries, some serious. There were, over the years from 1886 to 1932, five fatalities, three of which were tramways employees, one a child, and the other a young driver of a furniture van. The first two fatal accidents, involved steam trams.

3rd January 1889

In the first year of these, Abraham Bridge (aged 22) of Cloughfold, Rawtenstall, was driving a horse-drawn furniture van towards Accrington; near Colliers' Row (just above Harcourt Road). He heard a steam tram coming behind him, and drove onto the pavement to give the tram room to pass. Unfortunately, the front of the engine clipped the rear corner of the van, and spun it round. Bridge was holding the horse's head, and the sudden movement of the van made him lose his footing, and he fell to the pavement, where the front wheels of the van ran over his chest. The impact also broke one of the shafts, which penetrated his neck. He was taken to Accrington Victoria Hospital by horse ambulance, but was pronounced dead on arrival. The horse was slightly injured by contact with a wall, and gashed by the broken shaft, but was not seriously hurt.

1st July 1890

The second accident involved a $2^1/_2$ year old girl named Edith Blackburn, of Manchester Road, Baxenden. Her mother was in the habit of leaving the child with a neighbour, Mrs Cox, while she went to work. On returning from work on this day, she picked little Edith up from Mrs Cox, and took her home. Shortly afterwards, the child went out to play with her elder sister, who was on the opposite side of the road. Her mother warned her to look out for the trams, but a few seconds later she heard a tram bell ringing loudly, and rushed to the door, where she saw the child hit by the tram, and dragged under the skirting which protected the wheels. The tram stopped very quickly, and Edith's body was found on the road between the engine and the car. At the inquest, a weaver, Richard Hargreaves, who lived at Acre, told the coroner that he witnessed the accident. He ran to try and drag the child out of the way, but was too far off, and could not save her. He gave his opinion that the tram driver had no chance of avoiding the accident. A verdict of 'Accidental Death' was returned

Bumps and Scrapes

After electrification, four minor accidents occurred in Union Road, Oswaldtwistle, between October 1907 and April 1908. In the first one, car no. 2 was badly damaged on one side by a horse and cart backing into it. The cart was heavily loaded, and the damage to the car's panelling was considerable. The other three accidents were minor collisions between trams on the single line sections. Damage was slight, amounting to nothing more than dented or displaced dashplates, and there were no injuries. As a result of these, the system of light signals was introduced in 1908, to show drivers whether or not the single line sections were occupied, and there were no more collisions.

12th March 1916

This serious collision took place in fog, on Whalley Road, Clayton. Car no. 7, proceeding towards Accrington, had just left the Sydney Street loop, and in about fifty yards collided head on-with no. 15, travelling in the opposite direction. Visibility was very bad; only about ten yards. Both cars were moving faster than they should have been under the conditions. The platforms of both were badly damaged, no. 7's controller being displaced. The controller was a large metal box placed just inside the dashplate at the front of the car. This contained all the mechanism for driving the vehicle, with a handle on the top which on being turned, controlled the mechanism inside the box, and this increased or decreased the speed. A second, smaller handle was used to engage forward or reverse movement and also to switch out the mechanism if required.

Driver Crabtree on no. 7 was badly injured. He died, as a direct result of the accident, three years later, on 20th August 1919. Driver William Holland, on no. 15, suffered two broken legs, and on his recovery was deemed unfit for further driving duties, and was given a permanent job in the depot. The Town Clerk was deputed to interview Crabtree's family and come to some arrangement with them for compensation. This was done, and the matter settled amicably, though details of the agreement were not disclosed.

19th August 1918

Two years later there was a fatal accident in the Ellison Street depot. As well as pits under the track for examination of the car trucks and running gear, there was a system of overhead walkways, about 12 feet above the floor, for the convenience of cleaners, to deal with the upper decks. Some of the night duty staff were up on these gantries cleaning the cars, when one of them (who was not named) lost his balance, and fell head-first to the floor, being killed instantly. How this happened was never satisfactorily explained, but the most likely theory was that he had somehow over-reached himself, and lost his balance while cleaning the car windows. As he was in the middle of the car, he had no chance of grabbing the safety rails of the end balconies to save himself, and there were no projections on the car side that he could hold on to. The overhead walkways were judged to be as safe as they could possibly have been. As this occurred in war time, under Government instructions little was revealed in the press.

Fog Again

The last fatal accident occurred, again in fog, on 14th February 1930, at Rising Bridge, on the Rawtenstall route, only a few weeks before the line was to close down completely. Car no. 22 was hit head on by a Ribble bus (on the Manchester express run), and the front of the car was completely demolished, the controller being thrown through the door into the saloon. Driver David Murdoch was badly injured and died in hospital a few days later. The bus was alleged to have been travelling too fast under the prevailing weather conditions, and its driver, Walter Hope of Clitheroe was indicted for manslaughter. He was convicted but acquitted on appeal. Twelve passengers in the tram were injured by flying glass and splinters; none of them seriously. The Ribble Bus Company accepted full responsibility, and paid for the repairs to the tram.

David Murdoch was a well known character. A Scot, he was over six feet tall, and therefore had a little difficulty in driving some of the cars, especially the cut-down pair, nos. 11 and 24, as his eye level was behind the upper panels of the platform end. He was very popular both with the passengers and his workmates, and was given a special funeral. His coffin was conveyed to the cemetery gates in a single-deck car, suitably draped in black. From there, the coffin was carried the three hundred yards to the cemetery church on the shoulders of eight of his workmates in full uniform. Burnley Road was lined by hundreds of people, who came to pay their last respects. The Mayor, the Town Clerk, the Tramways Manager, and other council officials attended the funeral. A fitting tribute to a popular and respected public servant.

Eyup

A rather bizarre accident happened to no. 13 on 17th December, 1929. The morning was very cold. Descending the long hill in Whalley Road, with hand brake partially applied, when passing Owen Street, the car encountered a patch of ice on the rails. The wheels immediately locked, and the car began to slide. Releasing his brakes and applying plenty of sand, the driver, John James Entwistle, 34 years, of Higher Antley Street, attempted to get the wheels revolving again, but the car continued to slide at increasing speed. From the Castle Hotel at the bottom of the hill, the road was then flat for about two hundred yards to the junction with Burnley Road, and the driver was confident he could bring the car under control by then, but this didn't work either, though the speed did drop considerably. Near the junction a motor lorry loaded with timber was travelling slowly in the same direction. Its driver, seeing the tram bearing down upon him in his rear view mirror, attempted to put on speed to get out of the way, but was hampered by other traffic. The tram crashed into the rear of the lorry, and the lorry driver then applied his brakes and managed to bring both

Lined up by the kerb are Guy double-decker no. 132, off to Fern Gore and Guy Arab no. 3, now in traditional rather than experimental livery. The two photos. on this page were taken from almost the same spot, enabling us to notice the change of street lamps and the background architecture.

Outside Burton's tailor shop in Blackburn Road, no. 36 is displaying a blank in its destination box, so what service it is working is not known. It was one of four Leyland Tiger (TS8) buses delivered in 1938, long before route numbers were introduced. The registration number is confusing — it appears to be CTJ13, but is actually 83, the first figure being almost entirely obscured by the starting handle.

We are looking down St James Street about 1950. There's a bus at one of the three termini near to the library, so this bus is going to Huncoat, Blackburn or Burnley at that time. In later years the Blackburn and Burnley termini were moved. In the distance can be seen the old properties in Union Street. They are surrounded by hoardings and would soon be demolished to make way for the sunken gardens, which themselves would be filled in and The Arndale Centre built on the site.

The Peel St. terminus of the Fern Gore route, at the bottom of Infant Street, in 1972. Leyland Atlantean no. 175, built the previous year, is being overtaken by no. 30, a brand new Bristol RE8L single-decker on the no. 7 Pendleton Avenue circular route, which has just completed the U-turn out of the opposite side of the bus station.

vehicles to a stand. The front of the tram was smashed in, the driver was seriously injured, but recovered in hospital later. Four passengers were injured, with bruises and slight cuts from broken glass. At the enquiry, the lorry driver, Tom Castle, of Church Lane, Clayton, was highly commended for his actions in the collision, and the tram driver was adjudged to have done all he possibly could under the circumstances. The tram was repaired, and returned to service.

The Top Came Off

The worst tram accident in Accrington occurred late at night in Manchester Road on 11th November 1911. This was a collision between two Rawtenstall Corporation cars, on Accrington-owned track, at Harcourt Road loop. Rawtenstall car no. 14 was descending Manchester Road from Baxenden shortly before 11 pm when the armature winding of one of its motors suddenly failed, unbeknown to the driver. The Rawtenstall cars were fitted with the Raworth regenerative braking system. This was a highly technical and complicated system which cannot be adequately described here. Suffice to say that when coasting downhill with power shut off, the regenerative braking effect was lost. Consequently, the car rapidly accelerated, until at a speed approaching 25 mph, it derailed itself at the points of the Harcourt Road loop, where its sister car no. 11 was waiting. There was a sidelong collision between the two cars, both of which were completely derailed by the impact, no. 14 coming to rest within inches of a standard supporting the overhead wiring at the pavement edge. No 11 was thrown aside in the opposite direction, and no. 14's roof came off completely landing in the roadway between the cars. Both were extensively damaged. By a miracle, no-one was killed, though fourteen passengers in both cars received injuries of varying severity, mostly cuts and gashes from the broken windows. The most seriously injured was the driver of the stationary car, who received a gash five inches long in his chin, necessitating twelve stitches. Four passengers on the upper deck of no. 14 had a miraculous escape:- by all assessment of the crash they should have been killed by the roof coming off, but they suffered bruises and minor cuts. Householders rallied round to help the injured, many of whom were taken indoors and supplied with hot sweet tea, and their injuries attended to. Three local doctors also arrived soon afterwards.

A telephone call to the Rawtenstall tram depot appraised them of the accident. Within an hour, two further cars from Rawtenstall arrived with the Tramways Manager and a gang of workers, who proceeded to examine the wreckage and begin a clearance. They worked through the night, but it was not until 7 am the next morning that the scene was fully cleared. How all the debris was conveyed back to Rawtenstall is not clear. The two trams could run on their own wheels, but could not be driven, so they had to be towed somehow. The rest of the debris must have been taken in a wagon.

The debris was kept untouched in one part of the depot until it had been thoroughly examined by the Board of Trade Inspector, Col. Druitt, after which it was loaded into railway wagons and sent to the original builders, the United Electric Car Co. of Preston, who completely rebuilt the two cars.

Rawtenstall Roasted

Col. Druitt's report on the accident made tramway history. It effectively sounded the death knell of the regenerative braking system. He it was who discovered that the true cause of the accident was the failure of the armature winding of the motor, which cancelled the braking effect when current was shut off. Up to then, everybody concerned had blamed the accident on greasy rails. However, by painstaking examination of the wreckage, and the scene of the accident, the colonel proved it was an inherent defect on the electrical system of the car which was the culprit. He had some scathing remarks to make on the subject, and decreed that Rawtenstall must alter the system to the normal type immediately, and must fit magnetic brakes, which they did not have at that time. He condemned the regenerative braking system as unsuitable for use on hilly routes such as Rawtenstall had. His words were made more effective in that a few months previously a similar accident had occurred on the Halifax tramways, which were also very hilly. All over the country tramways which had relied on the regenerative braking apparatus were forced to convert their vehicles to the normal system as soon as possible. Rawtenstall did so, and in addition to fitting magnetic brakes, also fitted an additional clasp brake, operated by a large handwheel fitted concentric with the normal hand brake column on the platforms.

On the Buses

The first recorded accident involving an Accrington Corporation bus occurred on 6th November 1929, when a 10 year old boy was killed by a bus, near Church Bridge. He was rolling a barrel which was to be part of a bonfire on Nelson Square, and was apparently so engrossed in his task that he did not see the bus.

Accidents with the Accrington bus fleet were rare, and apart from a few individuals killed or injured by running in front of a moving bus, there were no serious collisions or other crashes. However, on five separate occasions between 1932 and 1982, a bus had its roof clipped off by making a wrong turn and going under a low railway bridge. The first two of these involved workmen's buses returning empty to the depot, but the other three were service buses. Luckily, injuries to passengers were not many, and were of a minor character, most of these on the upper deck being able to take evasive action. Three of these were under the same bridge, in Willows Lane, one was in Lonsdale Street, and the other in Blackburn – where no. 168, then a brand new bus, was on a private hire run, late at night. The other four buses involved were nos. 70, 82, 108 and 182. Only the first two had their roofs completely removed.

Strikes

The General Strike of early May 1926 lasted approximately ten days. It was called by the Unions in support of the miners, who had been on strike earlier, without any tangible results. Everything was supposed to stop working:- it didn't exactly turn out that way. As far as Accrington's transport was concerned, there was a great deal of upheaval, but in reality, some services continued throughout the whole period, but in a very tenuous and scrappy way. Some driver's and conductors on the trams (and the private buses) continued to work, but there were very few of them. A small number of civilians offered to work on a voluntary basis, and their services were accepted, mainly as conductors. A sort of tram service was maintained, mostly by single deck cars, with a volunteer driver, sometimes accompanied by a policeman, in case of attack by strikers — which happened in a few cases — but there was little, if any, damage done to the vehicles, though one or two drivers suffered minor cuts and bruises from sticks and stones. The services run were very erratic, there was no attempt at a timetable, the cars were operated as opportunity allowed, or on the whole, cars were few and far between. No attempt was made to run through services to Rawtenstall or Blackburn — the trams operated entirely on Accrington-owned track and not always as far as the regular termini.

On the whole, Accrington took the situation very well, there was not a great deal of lawlessness in the way of demonstrations and 'fisticuffs', but a few of the more militant workers made their presence felt, as might be expected. In the end, the strike fizzled out gradually, and as is common in these circumstances, the strikers ended up worse off than they were before.

Apart from the General Strike, the Corporation tramways and buses suffered the odd strike at intervals, usually on the subject of pay or working conditions All except one strike only lasted a day or so, the exception being one from the 6th to 11th November 1967, which started a lengthy 'work to rule' period until the 27th of the same month, when the situation returned to normal. Other strikes, lasting a day, or part of a day, were one instigated by the conductors on 12th July 1944, which lasted only a few hours, and a one-day affair on 14th August 1959.

I have reason to remember this last strike, for at the time I was working at Waterfoot. When I came out of work at 7 p.m. that night, I was informed that because Accrington bus men were on strike, buses to Accrington were not running beyond Lockgate, so I was faced with a weary trudge of a little under six miles from Lockgate — there was just no alternative! The strike was over next morning.

In 1938 Blackburn Corporation issued a plan for the unification of bus services in Accrington, Blackburn and Darwen – Accrington, after discussions, rejected this plan. The same plan was repeated by Blackburn in September 1942 and in December 1951, being rejected each time by Accrington.

One of the 1928 Dennis buses (no. 51?) is seen squirming its way through Green Haworth. Since it is empty, and shows 'Private' on the indicator, its purpose is not known. It may be on its way to pick up a private party, or on the other hand, it could be on a test run after attention to some defect or other in the depot. The route through Green Haworth was difficult, a narrow road with sharp bends and an appreciable gradient.

Leyland Bus no. 78 waits at the Clayton terminus by Mercer Park and The Forts Arms, for its departure time on the through run to Oswaldtwistle. It was one of a batch of eight Leyland TD1 buses bought in 1931 and was also one of the first to be fitted with a diesel engine experimentally in 1935. It was also the last of the TD1 buses to remain in service, not being withdrawn until June 1952. We see the driver and conductor in full uniform.

Seen in Peel Street, alongside the old open market, with its removable stalls and canvas covers, is one of the Guy Utility wartime double-deckers, in its finest condition, with upholstered seats, repainted in full livery, and fitted with a route number blind, the date being about 1956. The Gordon shelter was removed from this part of the market in 1953, and the end of the later bus shelter erected in its place can just be seen at the rear of the bus.

In 1932 the Regional Transport Commissioner debated the proposal for joint bus services between Accrington and Blackburn, which the latter did not want to share with Accrington. This had been a bone of contention for some time, but was not finally settled until 14th May 1932, when it was agreed for a joint limited stop service (Route 9). Blackburn was not keen, they were afraid of the effect it would have on the tram service. The stopping service (Route 46) did not begin until after the closure of the Blackburn tram service in 1949. It commenced on 4th September 1950, on the basis of five Blackburn buses and two Accrington to work it.

Seen here in Peel Street is no. 10, the last of the six Guy Arab single-deckers, of the series 5-10, which were purchased in 1948/9. They had 5-cylinder Gardner diesel engines but their performance did not seem to suffer at all from having one cylinder less than the double-decker. No. 10 is showing the route no.7, but the destination Oswaldtwistle; there is something amiss here. It should be no. 1 route. These six buses were withdrawn from service between 1960 and 1963, but no. 10 took on a new life, being altered in 1963 to a towing and breakdown vehicle. In this form it lasted a further twenty years, being finally sold – for preservation – in 1983.

Another class of bus which were 'foreign' to Accrington's fleet. Four of these double-decker Daimler CVD6 buses with Roberts bodies were purchased in 1950, at a reduced price. They were part of a cancelled order by Colchester Corporation, being left on the body-builders' hands, and they were glad to get rid of them. These buses were not popular – but with the drivers rather than the passengers – as with their fluid flywheels and semi-automatic gear boxes, they were difficult to get used to. However, they did put in 14 years of service before being disposed of. The location is on Paradise Street.

Tramcar Fleet Lists

Accrington Corporation Steam Tramways Company

9 miles, 4ft 0in gauge, steam traction, opened 5 April 1886, municipalised September 1907, closed 31 December 1907 (Accrington), 27 September 1908 (Haslingden)

Worked by 19 Thomas Green steam tram engines (1-9 of 1885, 10-14 of 1886, 15-16 of 1890, 17 of 1894, 18 and 6 (11) of 1898). Four similar engines (19-22) were purchased in 1901 from Blackburn Corporation. There were 14 top-covered bogie trailers by Ashbury (1-9 of 1886, 10-14 of 1887) and three Milnes trailers of 1891 (15-17?) Further trailers were bought in 1899 and 1900 from Blackburn Corporation, and probably two Falcon lower saloons in 1902 from Burnley.

Accrington Corporation Tramways (electric system) Livery: *Bright red and cream*

7.02 miles, 4ft 0in gauge, opened 2 August 1907, closed 6 January 1932. All cars were four-wheel double-deck unless otherwise stated. Seating figures shown thus 22/34 are for lower and upper decks respectively.

Car Nos.	Type (as built)	Year Built	Builder	Seats	Truck(s)	Motors	Controllers
1-4	Single deck	1907	Brush	32	Brush Conaty (a)	Brush 2 x 40hp	Brush HD2?
5-18 (note b)	Balcony	1907	Brush	22/28	Brush Conaty (a)	Brush 2 x 40hp	Brush HD2?
5,6(11)	Single deck	1908	Brush	32	Brush Conaty (a)	Brush 2 x 40hp	Brush HD2?
21,22	Balcony	1909	Brush	22/28	Brush Conaty(a)	Brush 2 x 40hp	Brush HD2?
23	Single deck	1909	Brush	32	Brush Conaty(a)	Brush 2 x 40hp	Brush HD2?
24,25	Balcony	1910	Brush	22/28	Brush Flexible	Brush 2 x 40hp	Brush HD2?
26	Balcony	1912	Brush	22/28	Brush Flexible	Brush 2 x 40hp	Brush 11D2?
27	Single deck	1912	Brush	32	Brush Flexible	Brush 2 x 40hp	Brush HD2?
28-30 (note c)	Single deck	1915	Brush	40	Brush MET-DK11 type bogies 2 x 40hp		DK DB1 K4
31,32 (note c)	Single deck	1920	Brush	40	Brush MET-EE DK30B type bogies 2 x 40hp		EE DB1 K4
38,39 (note d)	Enclosed	1915	Brush	32/44?	Brush MET-DK11 type bogies 2 x 40hp		K DB1 K4
40,41 (note d)	Enclosed	1920	Brush	32/44?	Brush MET-EE DK30B type bogies 2 x 40hp		EE DB1 K4
42,43 (note e)	Enclosed lowbridge	1926	Brush	26/34	Peckham P22	EE DK84 2 x 32hp	EE DB1 K44B

Notes:

a) The Brush radial trucks were later altered to Brush Flexible type.

b) Balcony cars 5 and 6 were renumbered 19 and 20 in 1908. Cass 9, 10 and 17 ran as open4op from 1917, but 9 and 10 received top covers again about 1928.

c) Cars 28-32 were sold in 1932 to the Llandudno & Colwyn Bay Electric Railway, becoming L&CBER 1-5 respectively.

d) Car 39 was sold in 1933 to Lytham St Annes Corporation for trial purposes, becoming Lytham 55. Cars 38, 40 and 41 were retained for possible sale to Lytham, but were sold in 1934 to Southend-on-Sea, becoming Southend 66-68.

e) Cars 42 and 43 were sold in 1931 to Sunderland Corporation, becoming Sunderland 19 and 20.

The Baltic Fleet arrives in Haslingden. The section from Baxenden to Haslingden centre opened on 27th August 1887. A tram depot was built in John Street, where four steam trams and trailer cars were stabled. The building on the left is the UnionFoundry which still stands today. Not so for the other buildings behind the steam trams, it is just an open space.

Sixteen years old Jeff Duckworth of Great Harwood, a keen bus spotter, captured these two Leylands for us. In Whalley's bus terminus, its conductor eyeing the front-loading Ribble bus pulling in behind, is no. 148, on the 231 service to Clitheroe in June 1961. On a sunny day, in May that year, no. 127 is running past St. Bartholomew's Church, Park Lane, Great Harwood on its way to Whalley.

ACCRINGTON BUS FLEET

1928 – 1986 (In Date Order)

Nos	Date	Reg. Nos	Chassis Maker	Chassis Type	Body Maker	Body Type	Sold	Notes
44,45	1928	TE5586/7	Dennis	G	Brush	B18F	1946-1950	A
50-53	1928	TE5582-5	Dennis	E	Brush	B32R	1940-1942	
54-57	1929	TE7867-70	Dennis	E	Brush	B32R	1945-1946	B
58,59	1929	TE9315/6	Dennis	H	Brush	L48R	1940	
60-65	1930	TF1505-10	Leyland	LT1	Leyland	B32R	1945-1952	
46-49	1931	TF4430-33	Dennis	EV	Brush	B32R	1944-1946	
66-71	1931	TF2964-69	Leyland	TD1	Leyland	H54R	1949-1952	
72,73	1931	TF3441, 3864	Leyland	TD1	Leyland	H54R	1948	
74-81	1931	TF4422-29	Leyland	TD1	Leyland	H54R	1947-1952	
82-85	1932	TF5760-63	Leyland	TD1	Leyland	H54R	1947-1951	
40-43	1932	TF6333/4, TF6394/5	Leyland	TS1	Leyland	B32R	1947	
86.87	1932	TF7399,7400	Leyland	TD2	Leyland	H54R	1951	
88,89	1937	CTC216/7	Leyland	TD5c	Leyland	H56R	1952	
90,91	1938	CTD242/3	Leyland	TD5c	Leyland	H56R	1952	
92,93	1938	CTJ81/2	Leyland	TD5c	Leyland	H56R	1952	
36-39	1938	CTJ83-86	Leyland	TS8c	Leyland	B32R	1955	
94,95	1939	DTE338/9	Leyland	TD5c	Leyland	H54R	1953	
44,45	1943	FTD180,209	Guy	ARAB3/6LW	Park Royal	H56RU	1957	
58,59	1944	FTD530/1	Guy	ARAB3/6LW	Massey	H56RU	1957	
96,97	1944	FTE51/2	Guy	ARAB3/6LW	Massey	H56RU	1958	
98,99	1944	FTE461/2	Guy	ARAB3/6LW	Massey	H56RU	1958	
100	1945	FTF530	Guy	ARAB3/6LW	Northern Counties	H56RU	1958	
101-107	1946	GTD481-87	Leyland	PD1	Alexander	H56R	1959	
108-114	1947	HTF821-7	Leyland	PD2/1	Leyland	H56R	1960-1962	
1-4	1948	JTF737-40	Leyland	PS1	Burlington	B35F	1965	
5-8	1948	JTE221-24	Guy	ARAB3/5LW	Guy	B35R	1960-1963	
9,10	1949	KTC614/5	Guy	ARAB3/5LW	Guy	B35R	1963	C
115-118	1949	KTC955-58	Leyland	PD1A	East Lancs	H56R	1964-1967	
119-122	1949	KTE977-80	Leyland	PD1A	Bruce	H56R	1965-1968	
123-126	1950	LTB204-07	Daimler	CVD6	Roberts	H56R	1964	
127,128	1951	NTD589,90	Leyland	PD2/1	Leyland	H56R	1969	
129-133	1953	PTE191-95	Guy	ARAB4/6LW	East Lancs	H58R	1969-1971	
134-137	1954	STE753-56	Guy	ARAB4/6LW	East Lancs	H58R	1969-1971	
14-16	1956	VTE778-80	Guy	LUF/6LW	Guy	B43R	1965	
138-141	1957	354-57 BTB	Guy	ARAB4/6LW	East Lancs	H58R	1971-1972	

Nos	Date	Reg. Nos	ChassisMaker	Chassis Type	Body Maker	BodyType	Sold	Notes
142-145	1958	321-24 DTB	Guy	ARAB4/6LW	East Lancs	H58R	1972	
146,147	1958	387,388 FTB	Guy	ARAB4/6LW	East Lancs	H58R	1974	
148,149	1958	383,384FTJ	Leyland	PD2/20	East Lancs	H59R	1974	
150-153	1959	825-828 KTB	Guy	ARAB4/6LW	East Lancs	H59R	1974,75	
154,155	1960	949/950 RTB	Leyland	PD2/20	East Lancs	H59R	1975	
156,157	1961	35,36 VTF	Guy	W2/6LW	East Lancs	H66R	1968	
158,159	1962	417,418 XTF	Leyland	PD3/1	East Lancs	H90R	1976	
17,18	1962	381,382 YTE	Leyland	PSUC1	East Lancs	B43F	1978	
19,20	1963	915,916 TF	Leyland	PSUC1	East Lancs	B43F	1978	
160	1963	914 TF	Leyland	PD3A/2	East Lancs	H70R	1976	
161,162	1963	9689/90 TJ	Leyland	PD3A/2	East Lancs	H70R	1976	
163,164	1964	CTB557/8B	Guy	ARAB5/6LW	East Lancs	H70R	1976	
165	1964	FTD 634B	Guy	ARAB5/6 LW	East Lancs	H70R	1978	
21-23	1965	KTC334-6C	Leyland	PSUC1	East Lancs	B43F	1978	
24	1965	RTD 506C	Leyland	PSUC1	East Lancs	B43F	1978	
166-169	1967	CTB166-9 E	Leyland	PD3A/2	East Lancs	H72F	1980	
25-28	1968	MTJ925-8 G	Bristol	RESL/6L	East Lancs	B47F	1982	
29	1969	STC 929G	Bristol	RESL/6L	East Lancs	B47F	1982	
170-172	1969	STB790-2G	Leyland	PDR1A/1	East Lancs	H78F	1981	
173-175	1971	CTC173-5 J	Leyland	PDR1A/1	East Lancs	H78F	1983	
176-179	1971	HTF176-9K	Leyland	PDR1A/1	East Lancs	H78F	1986-1988	
30-33	1972	OTJ357-60K	Bristol	RESL/6L	East Lancs	DP42F	1985	
180-181	1972	RTB797/8L	Leyland	AN68/1R	East Lancs	H78F	1989	
34,35	1973	OTF375/6M	Seddon	RU	East Lancs	DP42F	1984	
36,37	1973	BTF376/7L	Seddon	RU	East Lancs	DP42F	1984	
38	1974	STC 986M	Seddon	RU	East Lancs	C39F	1983	
182-184	1975	JBV818-20N	Leyland	AN68/1R	East Lancs	H78F	1989	
39,40	1975	YTB953/4N	Bristol	RESL/6L	East Lancs	DP42F	1986	
41,42	1976	OCW451-4P	Bristol	RESL/6L	East Lancs	DP42F	1986	
185-88	1976	PHG775-8P	Leyland	AN68A/1R	East Lancs	H78F	1989	
189-192	1976	URN326-9R	Leyland	AN68A/1R	East Lancs	H78F	1997	
43-46	1978	EHG43-46S	Leyland	PSUC3	East Lancs	DP42F	1997	
193,194	1978	KHG193/4T	Leyland	AN68A/1R	East Lancs	H78F	1997	
47,48	1978	NFR747/8T	Leyland	PSUC3	East Lancs	DP42F	1997	
195	1979	VCW195V	Dennis	DD110A	East Lancs	H78F	1997	
196,197	1979	VCW196/7V	Leyland	AN68A/1R	East Lancs	H78F	1997	E
198,199	1980	DBV198/9W	Leyland	AN68A/1R	East Lancs	H78F	1997	E
49	1980	GCK 49W	Leyland	PSUC3	East lancs	DP42F	1997	E

Nos	Date	Reg. Nos	Chassis Maker	Chassis Type	Body Maker	Body Type	Sold	Notes
101,102	1981	LFV 101/2X	Dennis	DD138A	East Lancs	H78R	1989	D
103,104	1982	SCW103/4X	Dennis	DD138A	East Lancs	H78R	1990	
105,106	1983	A105/6KRN	Dennis	DD138A	East Lancs	H78R	1990	
107,108	1985	B107/8UFR	Dennis	DD138A	East Lancs	H78R	1990	
50	1984	A50 LHG	Dennis	SD413A	East Lancs	DP42F	1997	E
51	1985	B51 XFV	Dennis	SD413A	East Lancs	DP42F	1997	E

Notes

A   Early in 1940 No. 44 was converted to a mobile canteen, and was withdrawn in 1950. No 45 was withdrawn in 1946, after having been used as a staff vehicle since 1935.

B   No.55 became a towing vehicle in 1946, and was disposed of in 1951.

C   No. 10 became a breakdown tender in 1963, and was sold for preservation in 1983.

D   Nos 101, 102 sold to Chester City buses (119,120)

E   These buses were absorbed into Stagecoach (Ribble) stock in 1997. All others existing at that time were sold.

Concerning body types, the following abbreviations are in common use: –

B   bus

C   coach

DP   dual purpose (bus type body, but with coach seats)

L   Lowbridge

H   Highbridge (denoting the overall height of double deck vehicles)

F   front entrance

R   rear entrance

Examples

B32R = 32 seater bus with rear entrance

72F = 72 seater double decker with high bridge type body and front entrance.

PLANT FOR SALE.

BOROUGH OF ACCRINGTON.

DISPOSAL OF OLD TRAMWAY RAILS.

The Tramways Committee of the Corporation of Accrington is prepared to receive tenders for the purchase of the old Tramway Rails comprised in the existing permanent way.

The rails are of the girder type, 6 inches section, 45 feet in length, original weight 92 lbs. per yard. They will be taken up, cleaned, and delivered on trucks at the Accrington and Baxenden Railway Stations respectively, as the work of relaying new rails proceeds. The estimated weight of rails for disposal is about 1,000 tons. Further particulars may be obtained on application at my office.

Sealed tenders, endorsed "Tender for Old Tramway Rails," to be delivered to me not later than Saturday, the 29th inst.

WILLIAM J. NEWTON, Assoc.M.Inst.C.E.,
Borough Engineer.

Town Hall, Accrington,
June 7, 1907.

ACCRINGTON CORPORATION

BUS ROUTE NUMBERS 1950 – 1985

    1   Oswaldtwistle (Black Dog) - Church – Accrington – Clayton (Forts Arms)
    2   Fern Gore – Accrington – Avenue Parade – Griffin – Huncoat (Station)
    3   Fern Gore – Accrington – Burnley Road – Griffin – Huncoat (Station)
   *4   Accrington – Baxenden – Haslingden – Rawtenstall – Waterfoot – Bacup
    5   Accrington – Church Kirk – Dill Hall – Accrington (Circular)
    6   Accrington – Dill Hall – Church Kirk – Accrington (Circular)
    7   Accrington – Willows Lane – Pendleton Avenue – Moscow Mill – Church – Accrington (Circular)
    8   Accrington – Church – Moscow Mill – Pendleton Avenue – Willows Lane - Accrington (Circular)
   +9   Accrington – Church – Intack – Blackburn (Express)
   10   Accrington – Hollins Lane
   11   Accrington – Laneside – Whalley Road – Accrington (Circular)
   12   Accrington – Woodnook – Accrington (Circular)
   13   Accrington – Burnley Road – Within Grove – Huncoat (Griffin)
   14   Accrington – Fern Gore – Green Haworth – Fielding Lane – Oswaldtwistle
   15   Accrington – Barnfield – Queens Road – Accrington (Circular)
   16   Accrington – Clayton – Rishton (Market Days only)
  +46   Accrington – Church – Intack – Blackburn (Stopping service)
  +90   Accrington – Oswaldtwistle – Blackburn Hospitals.
60-65   (Hyndburn Circular) Accrington – Oswaldtwistle – Blackburn – Great Harwood – Clayton - Accrington
70-75   (Hyndburn Circular) Reverse of 60-65
 #231   Accrington – Clayton – Great Harwood – Whalley – Clitheroe
 #251   Accrington – Clayton – Whalley – Clitheroe
 #243   Oswaldtwistle – Church – Dill Hall – Clayton – Great Harwood – Whalley – Clitheroe
 #264   Accrington – Griffin – Hapton Inn – Rosegrove – Burnley

* = Joint service with Haslingden and Rawtenstall Corporations
+ = Joint service with Blackburn Corporation
# = Joint service with Ribble Motor Service

Note – Hyndburn Circular services deviated in parts of Oswaldtwistle, Clayton and Great Harwood, each having a separate route number.

No. 94, a Leyland TD5 double-decker of 1939, standing at one of the three terminals in St James' Street, near the public library, bound for Huncoat. Only two buses were in this particular purchase, the other being no. 95. Both were withdrawn in 1953. They were the last buses to be added to the fleet before the war, when severe restrictions were brought into force by the War Ministry on the manufacture of bus chassis. The conductor is wearing a lightweight, summer-issue jacket, in contrast to the serge uniform he would be wearing in the Winter.

No. 16 has just left the Woodnook bus stop outside the fine Victorian Arcade in Church Street.

Accrington.

This steam tram is probably due to set off back to Baxenden from the town centre terminus. The engine, which we see at the front, would use the loop of track in front of the Town hall to turn round in order to pull, not push, the car. On the wall of the Commercial Hotel can be seen three clocks in a case. These would tell the public the time and what time the next tram would leave. This early 20th century photo shows us the gas and electric street lamps on the left pavement.

A message to all transport sinners from
An Anonymous Accringtonian

AT THE TERMINUS
A driver and conductor departed to their grave,
And stood before the Judgement Seat feeling very brave
But the Devil standing there rubbed his hands with glee,
"Come along you two", he said *"You belong to me.*
You're taking out this ghostly bus, across this endless sky,
And you'll have to get a whip out for this old bus to fly.
Your route is number one, Forts Arms to Black Dog,
And to keep yourselves on schedule – put down your flippin clog.
The running time I have cut, and a lot more stops you'll find,
and the waiting queues of passengers are those in life you left behind…
So, driver, you get cracking, and conductor, you take care,
Or I'll jab you with my pitchfork every time you miss a fare."

So drivers and conductors and clippies all take heed,
Mend your ways today and serve the public's need
Or on these ghostly buses you'll become a ghostly crew,
And lots of split-turns will be waiting just for you.

A circa 1960 view along Blackburn Road. No yellow lines or parking restrictions can be seen. The Church Kirk bus waits at its terminus outside Timothy Whites and Taylers chemists' shop. On the extreme right is Woods' Tobacconists shop.

So, in 1986 regrettably passed away in turn the steam trams, the electric trams, and finally the buses, leaving Accrington without any local transport of its own after a century of very successful working. Certainly under the present circumstances, this will never return, and the town must be obliged to outsiders for its transport.